PETER ALLISS'
MOST MEMORABLE GOLF

PETER ALLISS' MOST MEMORABLE GOLF

Peter Alliss
with Michael Hobbs

Illustrations by Roy Ullyett

Stanley Paul
London   Melbourne   Auckland   Johannesburg

Stanley Paul & Co. Ltd

An imprint of Century Hutchinson Ltd

62–65 Chandos Place, London WC2N 4NW

Century Hutchinson (Australia) Pty Ltd
16–22 Church Street, Hawthorn, Melbourne, Victoria 3122

Century Hutchinson (NZ) Ltd
32–34 View Road, Glenfield, Auckland 10

Century Hutchinson (SA) Pty Ltd
PO Box 337, Bergvlei 2012, South Africa

First published 1986
© Peter Alliss 1986
Illustrations © Roy Ullyett 1986

Set in Baskerville by
Tradespools Ltd, Frome, Somerset

Printed and bound in Great Britain by Anchor Brendon Ltd,
Tiptree, Essex

British Library Cataloguing in Publication Data

Alliss, Peter
Peter Alliss' most memorable golf.
1. Golf—History—20th century
I. Title II. Hobbs, Michael, *1934–*
796.352'09'04   GV963

ISBN 0 09 166050 5

Contents

Photographic Acknowledgement

For permission to reproduce copyright photographs, the author and publishers would like to thank Peter Dazeley, All-Sport, The Photo Source, Sports Photo-Graphics and Syndication International.

Introduction

Although I've been involved in the game of golf professionally for forty years, it is only in the last fifteen years or so that I've been a golf watcher. When you are a tournament player you see less than some might think of what the others are doing. That is why so many of my memories are of fairly recent happenings. I didn't, for example, see anything of the mastery of Hogan at Carnoustie in 1953 or Palmer at Troon in 1962. I was too busy trying to win, or at least do well, myself.

I have included a few memories of my own play but I have to confess that, unaided, I remember remarkably little. I've needed Michael Hobbs' detailed research into scores and reports of the time to nudge my memory, and more of the past does then come back. Otherwise a course record here and a tournament win there are utterly gone. I'm amazed when I listen to some of my professional colleagues reminiscing. They seem to have total recall of every shot they played, whether it be in an open championship or just a friendly fourball for 50p corners. My recollections of my own play, without prodding, are so few as to be laughable. A pistol held to my head might compel me to remember, say, fifteen or twenty splendid or horrid shots from my twenty years of competing as a professional and well over forty of simply playing the game of golf. Michael is much the same. He can remember and feel the odd long iron which felt right the moment club met ball, the tiny pitch struck to perfection, or long putt when judgement of line and strength were so good that whether or not the ball went into the hole was not really very important.

At the end of the 1969 season I won the Piccadilly tournament at Prince's, Sandwich. I had already given up international play after that year's Ryder Cup match at Royal Birkdale and, without a conscious decision, that was the end of my full-time competitive career also. I had already written and commentated on golf for a good few years, and that increasingly became what I did in life. Since then I have always felt very privileged to have been at almost every major golfing event throughout the world, and have seen most of the truly great achievements as they happened. Here, my recall is almost total and this is what this book is really about: the achievements of Jack Nicklaus in 1980 after a disastrous 1979 that seemed to write 'finis' to his career; the strange career of Ray Floyd; what went wrong with Tony Jacklin – and what went right also; the passion to win a major championship of Ben Crenshaw; how and why Gary Player became the greatest match golfer since Walter Hagen; the unprecedented feats of Peter Thomson in America in 1985; the grit and tunnel vision of Tom Watson and . . . well you'll find the rest in these pages. There is, I do assure you, also a mention here and there of Seve Ballesteros, for me the most complete player ever, and Bernhard Langer, equally remarkable, for once you start twitching putts it's with you for ever. Instead, Bernhard has become one of the best putters in the world. And many others. I hope you share my own taste for the unexpected, the quirky and the outright bizarre as well as simply superb golf when the heat is on.

Somewhere or other, I may also have spotted, without realizing it, the next superstar they feel so starved of in America, or a successor to Roberto de Vicenzo from South America, a new star amongst the Asians, a real successor to Peter Thomson . . . One could go on but, simply, José-Maria Olazabal may still be worth a thought, even if he's only won the European Tour qualifying school, had an outstanding amateur record and lost his first play-off in the Spanish PGA to a certain S. B., playing on his home territory at Pedrena in northern Spain.

I hope you enjoy the book and your other interests in golf. In the years ahead, there'll be plenty more moments to remember.

When What Couldn't Happen, Happened

Needing a last round in par or, indeed, coming to the final stretch knowing you have 'only' to par the last three or four holes for a tournament victory is one of the hardest tests of nerve in golf. In some ways, some may be surprised to hear, it can be more difficult than to produce a 66 to win. Here, the golfer has to go for his shots. If everything comes off, headlines are made and the player who achieves that score of 66 is justifiably proud.

If, however, he doesn't manage a magical round, there's no real cause for heart-searching and self-doubt. That sub-par round may have been the target but it was a very difficult one. To fail is hardly failure at all. On the other hand, any professional worth his salt knows that he ought to be able to produce par figures to win. A round of 75 in these circumstances is a total failure.

Such a failure is usually the result of lack of nerve – but not always. Take the case of Lee Trevino in the 1971 British Open at Royal Birkdale. He set out on his final round with a one-stroke lead over Tony Jacklin and 'Mr Lu' (Lu Liang Huan from Taiwan). Trevino began holing everything and reached the turn in 31. This gave him a four-stroke lead on Lu, with the rest of the field more or less nowhere. Lee began to enjoy himself and, as he later said, 'I almost forgot to win the tournament.'

Loss of concentration was the problem and led to a hook into sandhills at the 17th, and a 7 resulted in a relatively easy par-5 which cut his lead to a single stroke. In Trevino's case it all ended well. Even with that major error, he still needed only to par the last hole – and he did.

It was a different kind of loss of concentration that afflicted Arnold Palmer at the Olympic Country Club, San Francisco, in the US Open Championship of 1966. Palmer also 'forgot to win the tournament' because, as we shall see, he was thinking of something else.

At that time Palmer had been at the top of American golf since his first Masters victory in 1958. Since then he had added six more major championships to his record: three more Masters, a US Open and two British Open titles. He had also won no fewer than forty-two US Tour events. Besides his other great talents, some thought he was the finest putter ever seen. How confident the man was, always striking the ball firmly at the hole, apparently unconcerned about the three-, four- and five-footers he often left himself on the way back. It was all quite simple for Palmer in those halcyon days. You just took careful aim, locked knee against knee, kept your head still and ran your ball at the hole. In the five years between 1960 and 1964 he was always first or second on the US money list.

Suddenly, however, the great man began to falter. He suffered from a bad back and bursitis of the hip but, far worse, his putting declined from great to mediocre. Letters poured in to his Latrobe home offering all sorts of cures for what ailed him, and Arnold increased his collection of putters in the hope of finding the magic wand that would bring back the great days.

In 1965 he fell to tenth on the US money list, his worst result since being a second-year professional. However, he won the first event in 1966 and his putting seemed more confident. He was not the Palmer of old, but quite a consistent performer who had some very good days on the greens.

Although he came to Olympic in good heart, his first hole was not encouraging. Having missed this par-5 green with his second shot, he then thinned a wedge shot through the green and took 6, but immediately got back the lost stroke with a birdie on the 2nd. That was the kind of round he had, a mixture of birdies and dropped shots, but his 71 was a good score. Olympic that year wasn't particularly long, 6719 yards, but the rough was wiry, and every fairway on the undulating course was flanked by trees making the last few holes look like tunnels from tee to green. When Ben Hogan tied with Jack Fleck for the US Open in 1955, their four-round total was 287. Only two higher scores have won this championship since.

A few other players scored better than Palmer, but in the main they were the wonders of the day. There was a new marvel on the second day, Rives McBee, a twenty-seven-year-old assistant professional from Texas, just up to see the sights. He managed to score nine birdies round Olympic for a total of 64, which tied the US Open record.

As regards the outcome of the tournament, however, Palmer's 66 was obviously far more significant. It was the great man at his best, putting for birdies on every hole except one and only off the fairway once. Was it ominous, however, that Arnold had missed short putts on each of the last two greens?

At the end of the day, on 137, he led with Billy Casper, who had rounds of 69 and 68. Jack Nicklaus, the man Palmer feared most, was five strokes behind but playing well enough, having had two rounds of 71.

On the third day, Palmer and Casper were out together. It was to be the first of three days in each other's company. At the time, Casper aimed to fade the ball while Arnold had always been happiest playing with draw. He feared Casper, then in his best years, almost as much as Nicklaus. Both were faders and nearly every hole at Olympic favoured a left-to-right shot from the tee and into the small greens.

But Palmer, whatever his fears, had plenty of confidence. After six holes in that third round, he had taken a four-stroke lead over Casper. Errors then crept into his game and Casper drew level on the 13th. But Casper was not playing his usual steady undramatic game. He was in the rough seven times and hit only eleven greens in regulation figures. However good his putting, no golfer can scramble for ever. Casper faltered and was round in 73 to Palmer's 70.

At the end of the day it was a three-horse race: Palmer 207; Casper 210; Nicklaus 211.

On the final morning only one of those horses raised a trot over the more difficult first nine holes at Olympic. Palmer turned in 32, at which point he had a seven-stroke lead on Casper with Jack Nicklaus nine behind.

Palmer now began to think of other things. Surely he'd got the championship in the bag. He'd started the day with hopes of breaking the US Open record of 276, set by Ben Hogan at the Riviera Country Club in 1948. He only needed a round of 68 to do that and it was now well within his grasp – thirty-six strokes needed for the second nine. After the 13th, 191 yards, where he took 4 to Casper's 3, he needed to par the last five holes to break Hogan's record.

The 15th is as easy a short hole as you're likely to find, just 150 yards. However, Palmer wanted the cushion of a birdie. The flag that day was well over to the right side of the green, close to some bunkers. Casper played cautiously for the centre of the green while Palmer went boldly at the flag. His ball drifted a little too far right and he ended up in the sand. He played out quite well to nine feet and watched while Casper holed his putt for a 2 and then missed his. The Open record was just about gone and, unnoticed, Casper who had said on the 10th tee, 'You know Arnie, I'm really going to have to go now to get second place', had cut Palmer's lead to three strokes.

There were just three holes left to play. Did Casper have hopes of catching Palmer? I think not. Palmer, however, was beginning to have doubts. When interviewed later, he said, 'That's when I began to wonder. I knew what could happen.'

Faced with the 604 yards of the 16th hole, Billy Casper didn't exactly throw his cap at the windmill. He played a safe shot with an iron down the middle. Though a draw is Palmer's natural shot, he had come to Olympic hitting a straight ball. Because the course favours a left-to-right shot he had tried an adjustment here and there to see if he could fade the ball consistently. He could and that had been one reason for his good scoring: he was starting the ball down the left side of the fairway and drifting it back to the centre.

But the 16th was an exception, a dogleg to the left. Palmer would benefit if he reverted to his normal shape of shot. If he could draw a long one round the corner, he might get on in two. Whether he hoped to crush Casper's effort there and then or give himself a chance at the Open record I don't know. Perhaps simple pride of performance wouldn't let Palmer follow Casper's cautious iron shot from the tee.

Out came the driver. The attempted long draw was a pull that hit a tree some 180 yards out and dropped down into deep wiry rough. Palmer had over 400 yards still to go and then made the decision that was to cost him the 1966 US Open – or so it looks twenty years on. Instead of playing a safe shot back to the fairway he took a 3-iron which caught the long grass and went only about seventy yards, stopping in even deeper rough. Palmer now wedged to the fairway and then fired a wood at the green, which finished in sand. A 7 looked likely but he managed to get down in two more for a 6. Casper, playing for a par, was on the green in three and holed a good putt for a birdie 4. Now he was just one stroke behind and suddenly realized he could win.

On the 17th, a long par-4, Palmer again pulled into the rough and could not get home in two. Neither did Casper, but he took one putt to Palmer's two. Level.

The last hole at Olympic is a par-4, a drive and pitch of 330 yards or so. Palmer took an iron off the tee but again missed the fairway. From the rough he played a good wedge shot which just held the green. However, he was thirty feet from the hole and Casper half that distance after a good second shot. After his first putt it looked as if Palmer had lost the championship, for he was still six feet away and had to putt again because a continuous putting rule was in force that year. Was he going to leave Casper with the easy task of having 'two for the Open'. It was a massive pressure putt but Arnold willed it in. Casper, cautious to the last, didn't appear to go for his putt and tapped in a short one to tie on 278. Palmer was round in 71, Casper 68. In third place was Nicklaus, seven strokes away.

So Palmer had undoubtedly failed. Even so he'd had a very good championship and, with Casper, had finished with a total nine strokes below the mark set by Ben Hogan and Jack Fleck at Olympic eleven years earlier. Tomorrow was another day. Few believed they could cope with Arnold in a play-off over eighteen holes.

Palmer, apparently with confidence unimpaired, covered the first nine holes in 33. Although Casper was only two strokes behind at this point he had been getting his figures with difficulty. On the 11th, however, there was a two-stroke swing in Casper's favour. On the 13th he went into the lead, and was two ahead on the 15th tee. From this point on Palmer's errors were strangely similar to the day before. Again he missed the green on this par-3. On the long 16th, once more he pulled into the rough, hit a tree and again, scarcely credible though it may seem, tried to escape with that same 3-iron. This time his ball only went about twenty yards. The only change in the script from the previous day was that Palmer took 7 instead of 6, while ironically Casper did something he'd avoided in the first four rounds of championship play – three-putted both there and at the very next hole. But he was still three strokes ahead on the last tee and birdied the hole, to finish in 69 to Arnold's 73.

It was the third play-off for the US Open Palmer had been involved in over a five-year period. Amazingly, he was never to win or play off for a major championship again.

2

The Greatest Golfing David of Them All

Who won four British Opens but none of them when his greatest rival was in the field? And who won four US Opens, all of them *with* his greatest rival playing? The answer to my first question is Walter Hagen, who never beat Bobby Jones in the event and to my second, Bobby Jones, who always came out ahead of Hagen.

This might seem conclusive proof that Jones was the greater player of the two and I think he was – in strokeplay. In the art of matchplay, however, which some would say makes greater demands on resilience and the knack of summoning up an inspired thrust when it's most needed, Hagen was the greater of the two. His record was quite phenomenal. He fought his way through to four successive US PGA finals in the 1920s and won the lot. In play-offs after strokeplay ties, a man-to-man situation, he was able to say with none to contradict him: 'No one ever beat me in a play-off.' Hagen also played many challenge matches and few opponents came away with his scalp, even though many of these were hardly great occasions. He met Jones only once, in 1926, a challenge intended to 'prove' who was the best player in the world. Hagen won by 12 and 11. It was quite a thrashing for Jones though perhaps not quite as severe as it sounds, for the contest was over seventy-two holes and the difference between the two was simply that Hagen took a dozen putts less.

In the 1920s and 1930s it was possible to build a reputation for excellence at matchplay because there was so much more played, enough for clear superiority to emerge over the years. The demands of TV changed all that. The US PGA changed over to seventy-two holes of medal-play in 1958. In Britain the PGA Matchplay Championship, sponsored for many years by the *News of the World*, ranked second only to the Open Championship. It was a splendid event, but it began to falter and was taken over by a variety of sponsors. Sadly it hasn't been played since 1979. At last there are signs of a revival of matchplay tournaments. The US Tour ends its year with one, and a European counterpart begins in May 1986. For many years, however, it's been almost impossible to build a reputation as a matchplay golfer. True there is the Ryder Cup, but the results of individual matches soon fade. It is still remembered by quite a few that Brian Barnes beat Jack Nicklaus twice in a day in 1975, and Sam Torrance will long be remembered for being the man who earned the decisive point in the 1985 Ryder Cup match. Whom he beat may be largely forgotten already.

Only one event remains, the World Matchplay, boldly started by Carreras in 1964. In Britain it immediately became very popular indeed, an annual event second only to the Open Championship in its appeal to TV viewers and with as many spectators as the tree-lined course has room for. It was to be the stage where Gary Player established himself as the man who was best at beating anybody. Already recognized as a member of the so-called 'Big Three' when the event began, Gary's brinkmanship, stubbornness in refusing to accept that he was on the floor and the count had reached nine, and sheer delight in winning matches showed him to be the Hagen of the 1960s and 1970s.

It all started rather badly back in 1964. Gary began happily enough in the first round by despatching that year's US Open Champion, Ken Venturi, 4 and 3. With eight players in the field, he faced Arnold Palmer in the semi-finals. Player was confident. He had played Palmer thirty-seven times in exhibition matches, play-offs and

TAKE YOUR TIME SON. GARY PLAYER'S ONLY JUST GOT HIS SWING RIGHT—AND HE'S 50 YEARS OLD.

TV events and the two were all square with eighteen victories apiece and one tie.

But he was trounced. Palmer began the second eighteen of the thirty-six holes with an eagle, a par, and three successive birdies. Not long after he'd won by 8 and 6, a humiliating margin.

Player went away and thought about it. He vowed to himself that he would win the event the next year. But how to do it? A few years before Gary decided that he was conceding too much to other competitors in the US Masters because he hadn't the length to hit the par-5s at Augusta in two. He would have to make himself stronger. He did just that and won his first Masters in 1961, flying his second shots over water to the par-5 greens.

After Wentworth Gary came up with an obvious solution: he would have to make himself even fitter and build more muscle onto his five-foot-seven-inch frame. He hired a former Mr Universe and followed a programme which put on muscle just about everywhere. Perhaps, however, Gary was right when he came to feel that the best result, besides a couple of inches on his thigh, was more muscular protection around his nerves. It doesn't mean anything but Gary thought it did, and his confidence was increased; as vital a factor as anything in the world of golf.

At Wentworth in 1965 there were two British players to be disposed of if Gary were to meet Tony Lema, the 1964 Open Champion, in the semi-final. Player had to beat Neil Coles, and I had to go down to my friend Tony Lema. This is just what happened, and the scene was set for a match in which there was an amount of ill feeling fairly unusual in golf.

For a start the pair were opposites. Player, as he is only too willing to admit, was a bit of a bore with his talk of no alcohol, coffee or tea, plenty of nuts, bananas and raisins, the virtues for a golfer of supreme fitness and the benefits of religion. If his body was manufactured, so was his swing. Tony Lema, on the other hand, had a relaxed, flailing, elegant swing of rare beauty. But on the course he always seemed tense and nervous, rather like Bobby Jones, but had much of the same grace under pressure. He could use tension, not be destroyed by it. Off the golf course he had a very relaxed image, much enhanced when he bought champagne for the Press after a tournament victory. He was known thereafter as 'Champagne Tony'.

Lema's victory in the 1964 Open Championship, together with his US Tour wins, had made him a star. Gary Player felt that Tony resented the 'Big Three' Status of Palmer, Nicklaus and himself and knew Lema believed he was entitled to membership of that exclusive group. Lema had been saying there was really a 'Big Four'. There was also the matter of an important endorsement contract with Slazengers UK. They had dropped Gary and signed Lema instead.

The semi-final match which followed was the most enthralling I have ever seen, but I won't describe it blow by blow. That's been done by many others. Briefly, Player went into lunch six down at Wentworth, put in some practice to cure his hook and then came out and snap-hooked his first tee shot to go seven behind. With only nine holes of the thirty-six left to play Gary was still five down, but squared the match on the last and went on to win at the 37th. It has been called the greatest match ever. Player himself said: 'All through 1965, in the big events, I played in a state of enchantment, but this day, the day of the Lema match, was one of the most astonishing in my life. I have looked back on it and come to see in it a summation of so much of my character and personality, good and bad, so much of a reflection of the pattern of my life, that it has become for me a strange, unnatural distillation of all it means to be Gary Player, all that Gary Player is. Simply, it contains my whole life story.'

The next day, suffering little or no reaction, Gary went out and won the final against Peter Thomson by 3 and 2. The Lema match enormously increased his reputation as being 'the man who never gives up', but it certainly didn't mean he was thought of overnight as a great matchplayer. After all, there was still the memory of his heavy defeat at the hands of Palmer in 1964.

Nevertheless, Gary held the title of World Matchplay Champion, one he very much relished. The 1966 Championship was to give him recognition as the best matchplay golfer in the world.

The field was one of the strongest ever. In later years it has never been possible to assemble the best field, mainly because Jack Nicklaus and Tom Watson always turned down invitations to play. These were the players that year: Neil Coles, the year's leading money-winner in Europe; David Thomas, who had tied for second place in that year's Open Championship; Jack Nicklaus, Masters and Open Champion; Billy Casper and Arnold Palmer, winner and loser of the play-off for the US Open; 1965 Open Champion Peter Thomson; Roberto de Vicenzo, one of the greatest strikers golf has seen and 1967 Open Champion; and Gary Player.

Coles had reached the first final in 1964 and had been put out by Gary the following year. He was the holder of the *News of the World* Matchplay Championship and a Wentworth specialist, as he showed when he went round in the morning in 68 against Gary to be one up. The ding-dong struggle continued in the afternoon, but Player went suddenly two up when he birdied the 13th and 14th. Though Coles came back with a win at the 17th, a half at the last saw Gary through to the semifinal, where he faced Arnold Palmer, who had played phenomenally well against de Vicenzo. In the morning he was round in 66, and then did rather better in the afternoon – 31 for the first nine holes. A bewildered de Vicenzo shook hands ruefully, a loser by 10 and 8.

In the morning neither Palmer nor Player dropped a shot on any hole and both were round in 68. The afternoon's play was very even but, with a birdie on the 10th, Gary went two up. The decisive moment came on the 12th, a par-5 of about 480 yards and the easiest birdie opportunity on the course. Both had driven over the line of fir trees: Palmer was on the fairway, while Player's ball was well down in the rough. He could only hit a 6-iron. Palmer put his shot to the back of the green. The hole looked his when Gary's pitch came to rest a good few yards away, but Arnold putted up some nine feet short. Gary holed his putt and Palmer then missed to go three down with six to play. Par golf would almost certainly see Gary home. However, Palmer got a hole back when Player hooked his tee shot into a ditch on the 15th, and the 16th was halved in birdie 3s. Player two up.

With the honour, Palmer then thrashed an cnormous drive up the 550-yard 17th, but he overdid his normal draw and his ball finished in a garden out of bounds. Without pausing, he put down another ball and hit an even longer drive, down the middle this time and too late. All Gary had to do was knock three mid-irons from tee to green and two-putt for Palmer, at best, could only make a 5. The South African, however, took out a wooden club and launched a big hook which was out of bounds from the moment it left the clubface until it clattered into a fence and, what luck, remained in play by six inches. He just had room to swing at it left-handed with the back of his PING putter and succeeded in scuffling his ball back to the fairway. Now Gary did play conservatively, hitting a 6-iron and leaving himself with a wedge shot to the green. Palmer then rasped a 1-iron perhaps fifteen yards past the flag, just onto the back fringe. The match wasn't over yet. If Palmer could hole and Gary take three more to get down, Arnold would win the hole. Gary did take three, but Palmer failed with his putt so that the hole was halved in 6s and Player was the winner by 2 and 1. A scrappy end to a great match.

Afterwards, there was some good-natured banter about the rules of golf. On the 1st hole in the afternoon Player had driven first, though Palmer had in fact won the 18th in the morning round. Later, Palmer had teed off a second time when driving out of bounds on the 17th before Gary took his tee shot. And that shot with the back of his PING putter from Gary on the same hole. Was it legal? Didn't the rules state: 'The clubhead shall have only one face designed for striking the ball, except that a putter may have two such faces if the loft of each is substantially the same and does not exceed ten degrees.' A PING certainly doesn't have two faces 'designed for striking the ball' but it does have a thin bottom edge, which must have been what Gary used.

I leave it up to you, and mention these matters solely because this chat about possible breaches of the rules came before a major rules incident the next day.

Player had disposed of the great Palmer, who was at the top of his game. In the final he would meet the other member of the 'Big Three', Jack Nicklaus, perhaps in even more awesome form and still at the time in his career when he could propel a golf ball like an artillery piece.

In the first round Jack had disposed of David Thomas by 6 and 5, having gone round the West course in an estimated 64 in the morning without a 5 on his card. He had continued by dominating Billy Casper in the morning with a 67 to the US Open Champion's 73. Casper had given him a run for his money in the afternoon, however, firing off five 3s in the space of seven holes and completing the first nine in 32. This got him back to only two down. Later he was only one down with two to play, but whereas Nicklaus played a driver and 1-iron, both magnificent shots, to the 17th, Casper played safe on this dangerous hole – and stayed safe enough but lost both hole and match with a 5 to Jack's 4. Casper had won the US Open playing cautiously against a Palmer going for everything. It hadn't worked this time.

Nicklaus went into the final the hot favourite, but Player took an early lead. At the 9th, a long par-4, his tee shot was down the middle and Nicklaus followed with a hook which nearly finished out of bounds and in a ditch. He picked and dropped under penalty. Trouble with the rules lay immediately ahead. Jack looked up after his drop and noticed an advertising hoarding which he claimed would interfere with his shot. He asked the referee, Colonel Tony Duncan, for a ruling. Nicklaus felt he could drop again where he would not be obstructed. Duncan refused, so Nicklaus asked for a copy of the tournament local rules, which he was given. After reading the relevant passage, Jack still felt he was entitled to a drop without penalty as the hoarding was a temporary obstruction and on his line to the hole. Duncan kept to his ruling and moved off. Jack gave his ball a whack with a wedge and was still in the rough while Player was on the green in two. He conceded the hole, to go two down. On the next tee Colonel Duncan asked Jack if he'd like a change of referee. Nicklaus said he'd like someone who knew the rules, and in due course Gerald Micklem took over.

In my opinion Nicklaus was right but so too was Duncan, thinking that Jack would have gained an unfair advantage if he were allowed to move to a far better position. Was it against the 'spirit' of the game? The referee has a very difficult job, needing to know R and A and USGA decisions on obscure points of the rules, as well as the complex rules themselves. Being excellent golfers, as were both Duncan and Nicklaus, is certainly no guarantee as to rules expertise.

Today referees are appointed because of their knowledge of the rules of golf, but in the past they were there because they were good players and expected to know all. Take the example of my Ryder Cup match against Jim Turnesa in 1953 when the referee was Laddie Lucas, then a recent Walker Cup captain.

On the last hole (by coincidence this match was also at Wentworth) Turnesa's tee shot soared away into trees on the right. Lucas, having had no ruling to make all day, sauntered into the woods towards Turnesa's ball. Then he overheard two knowledgeable-looking spectators saying: 'If it's in that ditch and there's water in it, it'll be interesting to see what the referee makes of it. He may well rule that it's a lateral hazard.'

Lucas confesses that a sudden chill spread through his

body. He didn't actually know what a *lateral* water hazard was anyway. There was no chance that he'd be able to make a correct ruling with regard to dropping from lateral as opposed to 'normal' water hazards. He did the sensible thing – fled the scene, trying to give the impression that he really ought to have a look at that fellow Alliss' ball in mid-fairway. My God, he was thinking, please don't let them shout out for me!

They didn't, for Turnesa wasn't, as far as Laddie or I know, in the ditch but it was some weeks before Lucas could bring himself to consult the rules. When he did, he read as follows: 'A water hazard is any sea, lake, pond, river, ditch, surface drainage ditch or other open-water course (whether or not containing water) and anything of a similar nature.'

Later, comes: 'A lateral water hazard is a water hazard or that part of a water hazard so situated that it is not possible or is deemed by the Committee to be impracticable to drop a ball behind the water hazard and keep the spot at which the ball last crossed the margin of the water hazard between the player and the hole.'

Yes, any fool can understand the rules of golf.

Today we've become used to the tantrums of tennis players who apparently destroy their concentration in furious disputes with the umpire and then go on to serve out a love game. But we were innocents back in 1966. Surely Jack Nicklaus, having knocked that wedge shot along in the rough, should have lost the next several holes, particularly after the words he'd exchanged with Tony Duncan on the 10th tee. But no, he's made of sterner stuff. He birdied the next two holes to level the match.

On the 13th he lost his ball, and Gary then birdied the 14th to regain his two-hole lead. Shortly afterwards, Jack gave his new referee another problem. At the 17th he sliced his tee shot and hit a steward policing the edge of the fairway on the head, from where his ball careered away into a car park. Another ruling was very definitely in order, and Nicklaus was told he could drop his ball at the point where the head had been struck. He still lost the hole in 5 to 4, and the next also, to go to lunch four down. Player, uninvolved in any of the incidents, was round in an approximate 67; Nicklaus quite a few more.

In the afternoon both played the first nine in 33 and halved the next three holes. With Jack's chances running out at four down, he then hooked at the 13th and had still not regained the fairway after two more shots. Five down. And that was more or less that. On the par-3 14th he went for his 2 and then missed the return. Gary Player was World Matchplay Champion for the second time.

In successive years he'd won the impossible match and gone on to the title, and then beaten both of his fellow members of the 'Big Three' club in the 1966 event.

The years that followed did nothing to diminish Gary's reputation in matchplay golf. In finals he beat Bob Charles in 1968 and Jack Nicklaus again in 1971, followed by Graham Marsh a couple of years later with lots of derring-do from bunkers in extra holes.

Only in 1985 did he cease to get an automatic invitation. He may never play in the event again, but surely he proved himself the matchplay golfer of the 1960s and early 1970s as Seve Ballesteros has of the 1980s.

3

Magical Moments

I really think golf is the strangest game of the lot. For instance, how many 66s I've had when hitting the ball fairly poorly or 72s when my play through the green has been just about all I could ask of it, but not a putt would drop. Then there's the luck of the bounce and how the ball runs as well. It's so easy to hit an iron shot and say to yourself, 'It's in the hole!' But no, you catch a hard spot and finish at the back of the green with three putts staring you in the face. Of course, the opposite happens as well. A poorly struck shot often pitches short and, with less backspin than usual, runs much closer to the hole than you deserve. Perhaps things even out in the end.

I don't think I've ever played a round of golf without error when luck also ran my way throughout. Bursts of several holes, yes, but never a delightful eighteen of them.

Perhaps the most remarkable round I ever played was in my mid-twenties on the final afternoon of the 1957 Open Championship at St Andrews. At that time I didn't like the course at all well, and my first three rounds of 72, 74 and 74 had left me nine shots behind the leader, Bobby Locke. Before the championship began I had rather fancied my chances, but when the tapes went up my putter just didn't work well enough.

But a Spalding 10-iron certainly did that final round. I used it for my second shot to the 1st hole, hit the pin and finished no more than an inch away. I swear if it hadn't been leaning towards me, my ball would have dropped.

18

On the next hole, 411 yards, I did rather better, holing out for a 2. Well, that was an encouraging start, three under par with two holes played. I immediately had chances to make the Old Course feel rather silly, missing putts of five or six feet for birdies on the next two holes and did much the same for the remainder of the first nine – birdie putts all the way and none dropped.

On the 8th, however, 178 yards, my tee shot wasn't particularly good and I was some forty feet away when I putted. In it went!

With all those chances going begging, I reached the turn in 32. It really could have been 25.

I birdied the 10th, holing a good putt, parred the 11th and came close to holing out once again with my 10-iron on the 12th, 316 yards. I hit the pin first bounce and my ball spun around the hole, but didn't drop. Only a birdie but I was six under par and, surely, no longer nine strokes behind Bobby Locke.

No sooner had the thought come to me than I dropped my first stroke, taking 5 on the 425-yard 13th. I parred the next, however, and then missed birdie putts from around three yards on the 15th and 16th. I missed the green with my second shot at the Road hole, and took a pitch and two putts to get down for a bogey 5. I looked to have made up the ground on the last when that Spalding 10-iron had me no more than four feet from the hole, but I missed that one too.

My 68 missed equalling the course record by one stroke but what might have been! With a putter up to the mark, perhaps 25 out and 32 back. Yes, 57, a record that would still look unbeatable on any big course today and my name would have been on the trophy. After all, I needed 'only' a 60 to beat the great South African.

I had quite a similar round at Troon a few years later in the 1962 Open Championship. Again I was in good form and thought I had a good chance (no one could know how well Palmer was going to play) but Peter Thomson, unwittingly, upset my confidence during a practice round. He said he thought I ought to get rid of my driver. I was making my swing fit the club rather than find one that suited me. I knew this was nonsense because I'd been using the club successfully for many years. I never even gave my driving a thought. You just fired it down the left side of the fairway and watched your ball drift back into the middle. Alas, almost instantly my pretty fade became a wild slice at times, and I had no real confidence when I stood to the ball.

That was the main reason for my 77 in the first round. Though the course was so hard that the wild bounces made it almost unplayable and the greens were in poor condition, a 77 was still very poor and concentrates your mind on thoughts of qualifying, not winning. In fact, I hadn't played badly. It was just that any shot which was only moderate seemed to cost me a stroke. If I missed a green I didn't seem able to get down in two more, and my moderate shots were always punished rather severely.

Of course, it is always possible to win after a poor first round. Think of Curtis Strange, who could well have won the 1985 US Masters after beginning with an 80. My thoughts, however, when I started out to play my second round were just on qualifying for the thirty-six holes of the final day.

You must make a good start at Troon because the first three holes ought to be just a drive and pitch. I began by getting my drive away well, and then pitched to about six yards and holed the putt. I was closer than that on the 2nd, but missed the putt before getting my second shot just about dead on the next hole. Two under and then three under, with a 4 on the 4th, a par-5. The 5th was a par-3 of over 200 yards, but I hit my 4-iron reasonably close and had no trouble in making a par.

This was beginning to feel very good. I had no trouble with the 6th, over 580 yards and the longest hole in Open Championship golf. There was little chance that day of getting up in two, particularly as there are vast bunkers in a depression short of the green. I felt my par was good enough and another followed at the 7th, another drive-

and-pitch hole where I came close to a 3.

Then came my first error of any kind on the Postage Stamp, that little par-3 of 120 yards or so which ought to be so easy but there's always the fear of skittering to and fro in the bunkers that encircle the green, as Arnold Palmer was to do in a later championship, running up a 7. My tee shot was short and left. Although I was only a few feet off the green, the hole was a dozen yards away. But I now had my first piece of luck and holed out from there. Four under and, with a par at the 9th, out in 32.

All things were beginning to feel possible, but I kept my excitement in check. The bush telegraph was working by this time and my gallery had grown to several hundred. I responded with perhaps my best shot so far. On the 10th I hit a beautiful 6-iron approach that settled about four feet from the hole and got the putt. Now for the Railway hole, almost unplayable that year, with Jack Nicklaus, who was playing his first championship, getting into double figures.

The main trouble was the tee shot across the angle of the dogleg to a narrow strip of fairway which was bone hard and just about impossible to stay on. But my 2-iron did, and I followed with another of the same just short of the green and then chipped and single-putted. Six under.

On the 12th, my good drive finished in a grassy hollow and I had to manufacture a shot. I was a 4- or 5-iron away from the green, but I had to get the ball up quickly to clear the bank in front of me. It had to be a high hook with a 7-iron where I wanted to clip the side of a sandhill short of the green and get a kick on towards the flag. The shot came off exactly as I'd pictured and I nearly birdied the hole.

No problem at all on the 13th. A perfect drive followed by a good pitch pin high about five yards away, and a putt which needed one more turn for another birdie. Still six under.

The 14th was a 175-yard par-3 and I had my doubts about clubbing, but eventually settled on a 6-iron which went off a bit too well. However, I chipped back to about a yard. That was all right – until I missed the putt.

The 15th is 450 yards or so and was playing into a crosswind, blowing from right to left. I allowed a little too much and my ball settled well down in semi-rough along the right. From there I hit a 5-iron as hard as I could and my ball flew out high with a little hook on it, finishing just off the green. I decided to run my ball at the hole, chipping with quite a straight-faced club, but perhaps I didn't quite have the feel of the shot. I struck it indecisively and, of course, finished short and couldn't save my par with a good putt.

It was all beginning to slip away from me, but I got a good drive away on the 16th, long and dead straight. It looked as if I could be home in two on this long par-5. When I reached my ball, however, it was lying a little tight. I decided to be sensible and not go for the green but play up short and left, hoping to make my birdie with a little pitch and one putt.

In getting my ball up from that tight lie, I put some cut on it and, instead of finishing where I'd aimed, my ball drifted right – and into a cross bunker, ninety yards or so short of the flag. That length of bunker shot is always difficult, but I should still have got my par-5 from there.

When I reached my ball, however, it was in a horrid place, half-buried and well under the bunker face. Just getting it out was going to be no small problem. I opened the face of my sand iron and gave a great smash at the ball. At least I got it out, but only moved it forwards a few yards. Although from there I played a good wedge to about eight feet I still didn't manage the putt, so that was a 6 on a hole I hoped to birdie.

Three holes played, three strokes dropped to par and the last two holes a par-3 of over 220 yards and a difficult par-4. However, with my little world falling apart, I managed to pull myself together and parred them both.

It was a round of 69, the best of the championship at the time. The congratulations poured in, but I had a sour taste about it all. I had got myself into such a good position, where I ought to have been able to challenge for the lead. Later my round was equalled by the inevitable Arnold Palmer. The great man had just about played my round in reverse. He took 37 to the turn and then roared home in 32, so we had a 64 between us.

.The next day he really turned it on with rounds of 67 and 69, and was champion by six strokes from the steady Australian Kel Nagle. In third place, Brian Huggett and the American Phil Rodgers were another seven strokes behind. I played out the championship steadily, but with no more inspired moments and finished eighth, left with a few dreams of all that might have been.

Usually good scoring at golf is very much a matter of avoiding disasters, and I hadn't done that in my second round at Troon. The good shots can take care of themselves. Luck can, of course, vary tremendously. I can recall rounds of 72 which could well have been in the mid-60s but for a bad bounce here and there. Of course it works the other way as well, and I've had very good scores which I didn't fully deserve when my putter was a magic wand. That's why when commentating on golf I try to avoid saying that such and such a player's 65 was brilliantly played if I haven't seen all the shots – which we never do. It's safer by far just to talk about the *score*. The lucky player may have hit every tee shot off the fairway, but always found a good lie or bounced back from a tree. Nearer the green he may have thinned a shot and clattered into the flag, holed three chip shots and four long putts to save par.

Most of my other memories of really good golf are to do with my play through whole tournaments and not short bursts of miraculous scoring. The best golf I ever played was probably in the old Esso Golden tournament. This was always played at Moor Park, and lasted from 1961 to 1967. It was a matchplay event, a round robin with a select field, and everyone played everybody else over eighteen holes.

The weather was very good, my driving was excellent

and all the four-footers went straight into the middle –
and not a few long ones as well. With my final match still
to play, I was out of reach. I lost only to Christy
O'Connor, who finished with a couple of birdies and
halved with Kel Nagle after being dormie two up. My
final total of 25 points was a record for the seven years
the event lasted. I never relished playing in front of
spectators, but it didn't bother me for these few days. No
one moved when I was at the top of my backswing or had
to be asked to give me a little more room when I had a
tricky little pitch shot to play. The dogs didn't bark and
the birds sang quietly.

The best sustained spell of golf I ever had was several
years before, in 1958. It all began in the Open Championship at Royal Lytham and St Anne's where I had
steady rounds of 72, 70, 70 and 73 while putting none too
well. I finished seven strokes behind the champion, Peter
Thomson, who was taken to a play-off by David
Thomas.

Shortly after, I finished fifth in the Belgian Open and
fourth in Germany before going on to Varese for the
Italian Open, my first appearance in that country. The
course was a new one and not in very good condition.
There'd been heavy rain and it was all rather a question
of trudging round through the mud. The greens were
difficult and many were the tales of three-putting. Young
Alliss kept his mouth shut on this score. I'd been given a
tip before the championship began that, whatever it
might look like, all the greens sloped away from an old
hotel on a mountain top a few miles off. When faced with
a putt I wasn't sure about I just looked for the hotel and
then knocked it straight into the middle. I won by ten
strokes.

On to Puerta de Hierro, Madrid, for the Spanish Open
and a course in very different condition. This one was
bone hard and playing very short. My length from the
tee would be very little use and I began thinking that this
just wouldn't be my tournament. The best putter would
win.

At the halfway stage I was a few strokes behind the leader, but a 67 in the morning of the final day put me right in contention, just a stroke behind. In the afternoon I three-putted the 2nd and then was very unlucky on the 11th. There was a little bush in the middle of the fairway which you couldn't hit if you tried all week. My tee shot was unerring, however. It flew straight at it and stuck there. That hole cost me a 6. The rest of my card was virtually all 3s. I was round in 62 for another ten-stroke victory. The game of golf was beginning to feel easy. Take aim and fire and the ball did as it was told.

With two national championships under my belt it was onwards to Estoril for the Portuguese Open Championship, again over a course that didn't suit power play.

This time I jumped straight into the lead by two strokes with a round of 63, but began my second round with a 7 when my pitch came down on a very hard spot and bounded on through the green and out of bounds. The only thing you can do after that kind of bad luck is put it out of your mind – if you can. This time I managed it, and in fact had six 3s during the rest of the first nine and I came in with a 65. Although it was a low-scoring championship my last two rounds of 69 and 67 saw me home fairly comfortably, but only by what now seemed the rather narrow margin of three strokes.

And that was more or less the end of the season when I felt I could go on doing it for ever. In the world golf scene of today, I would have caught the next jet for wherever golf seasons were still on – Japan or Australia, perhaps.

I'm often asked what was the best round of golf I've seen at close hand, going round the course as a playing partner. The one that most sticks in my memory isn't something in the low 60s, and in fact it contained some rather poor golf. Bobby Locke was the player.

His start on the West course at Wentworth could hardly have been worse. At the 1st (which though now a very long par-4 was then a not difficult par-5) he began with a drive into trouble and an awful pushed second shot into more. It all added up to a 7, and he then three-putted the short 2nd hole. At the 3rd he met trouble with that bank in the middle of the green. His second was on, rolled towards the flag and then came back down again. He used his putter for his third shot. That climbed the bank towards the hole, hesitated, and then came back again to his feet. Most dispiriting. Bobby took 6 in the end, so that was a start of 7, 4, 6, against par of 5, 3, 4 – five over after three holes.

He said not a word to me and his expression and behaviour didn't change. Locke, a professional golfer in every way, just got on with the job in hand. He hardly made a mistake thereafter, when so many would have given up. Soon he was reeling off the pars and also getting the odd stroke back. On the 14th he had a 2, and at last allowed himself to speak to me. 'You know Peter,' he said, 'I don't think I've ever been so shaken in my life. That was certainly the worst start I can remember having.' He finished with more birdies on two of the last four holes for a round of 71, then three under the par. Peter Thomson and Gary Player learned a great deal about the mental side of golf from Bobby Locke. So did I that day.

4

Ryder Cup Memories

Alliss connections with the Ryder Cup go right back to 1929, the first year the event was held on British soil and still a couple of years before I was born. My father, Percy, was in the ten-man Great Britain and Ireland team but wasn't given a game. Perhaps there was less trust in youth in those far-off days, but it's ironic to think that if my father had been sent into the firing line the young Henry Cotton might have been the one to drop out.

For the next match in America in 1931, neither Cotton nor my father were qualified to play. Cotton was based at the Waterloo Club in Belgium and my father at Wannsee outside Berlin. The PGA had introduced a rule by which only home-based players were eligible. It was short-sighted, I think, and cost us our two best players and perhaps the match as well. Even today we still haven't found a system that ensures that all the best European players take the field, but perhaps we are coming closer. The idea of a world money list is developing, and perhaps both we and the Americans will use that eventually.

My father went over to America, however, to report the match for a newspaper. He took the opportunity to play a few tournaments, including the Canadian Open where he tied with the great Walter Hagen and so nearly became the only man to beat Walter in a play-off. He didn't lose until the 37th hole. What a marathon!

With the rise of Adolf Hitler, my father decided to

return to Britain and so was eligible for the 1933 match at Southport and Ainsdale. Partnered by Charles Whitcombe in the top foursomes the match with the best American pairing of Hagen and Gene Sarazen was halved. We led after the first day by 2½ to 1½.

For the thirty-six-hole singles matches on the second and final day my father was out more or less in the middle of our line-up, and a vital position it was to prove.

In three of the first four thirty-six-hole matches things began to go the Americans' way with Sarazen, Hagen and Craig Wood all winning and Abe Mitchell scoring the only point for Great Britain.

Then came my father, facing Paul Runyan, a man whose golfing talents were almost in reverse to his own. Runyan was nicknamed 'Little Poison' because of his prowess with the putter. As the climax of their match approached, it was clear that the Americans had drawn level and were thought the stronger at the bottom of the order by most pundits. However, my father won 2 and 1 and Arthur Havers, the 1923 Open Champion, beat Leo Diegel by 4 and 3. Unfortunately, Charles Whitcombe went down to Horton Smith 2 and 1.

There followed one of the most memorable finishes to all Ryder Cup encounters. Syd Easterbrook, a big Devonian based at the Knowle Club in Bristol, faced Denny Shute, winner of the British Open that year. On the tee of the 36th hole, 363 yards, with both their match and the Ryder Cup position all square, alas, Syd drove into a fairway bunker. Was all lost? No, the American immediately did likewise and both took three to reach the green. Shute three-putted from a dozen yards or so and Syd Easterbrook was left with a three-footer 'for the Ryder Cup'. In it went and Great Britain had won the Ryder Cup by a single point. Easterbrook was a hero and should have been made for life. Indeed, that same year he came within a shot of tieing with Shute and Craig Wood for the Open Championship. Later he turned against golf and announced he hated the game, and went on to run a pub and interest himself in greyhound racing.

Up to 1933 there had been no reason to doubt that golfers this side of the Atlantic could hold their own with the Americans. This was to change, and that victory at Southport was the last for many years.

The Cup passed back to American hands in 1935, but my father again gave a good account of himself. Playing with Alf Padgham he went down heavily 6 and 5 to Henry Picard and Johnny Revolta in the first-day foursomes but in the singles beat Craig Wood by one hole, the only one of our eight players to win his match.

When the match returned to home soil in 1937, again at Southport and Ainsdale, hopes for a British victory were high. After the foursomes on the first day, the score was USA 2½, Great Britain and Ireland 1½, my father and Dick Burton defeating Henry Picard and Johnny Revolta in the final match. After the first four singles matches, the two sides were level but our last four players all lost.

In what was to prove his last Ryder Cup match, my father again went out fifth, facing Gene Sarazen, a great player but one for whom my father had only limited respect, thinking he was a relatively poor striker of the ball.

What a struggle it was. Sarazen opened up with a 2 and played the next four holes in 4, 3, 4 and 4 to be four up. Was all lost? Not a bit of it. Big swings of fortune are always on the cards in singles over thirty-six holes. At the turn my father had got back to only one down and they were level on the 18th tee, Sarazen three-putting that green to go to lunch one down. After nine holes in the afternoon, my father looked to have the match almost in his pocket. He reached the turn three up, but then lost three in a row. Then came a disaster at the par-3 15th. Sarazen overclubbed his tee shot and ran up a slope at the back of the green. It ought to have left him a very tricky chip back. However, his ball came to rest on a woman's lap. She certainly didn't wait for a ruling and, no doubt in a dither, jumped up, shook her shirt and out came the ball, which rolled back down the slope to some eight yards from the hole. Sarazen rode his luck and holed for a 2. Alliss one down.

The next hole was halved, and on the 35th of the match Sarazen laid my father a stymie when he chipped up to about a foot. (In matchplay a player could not, as now, have an opponent's ball marked if it lay between his own and the hole.) However, there was just a chance that my father, if he judged pace and borrow to perfection, could shave past Sarazen's ball and maybe just topple into the hole from the side. He did just that. Sarazen later wrote, 'It was the greatest competitive putt I ever saw.' We Allisses could hole them sometimes! Even so, my father still went to the last one down and, when both players missed medium-length birdie putts, that was the way the match ended.

By this time my father was forty years old and, although picked for the 1939 team, the Second World War meant there were no more Ryder Cup matches until 1947. By then he was fifty and too old to be considered. It was perhaps as well he didn't go to Portland, Oregon, for we received a most humiliating defeat, coming home with only one point, scored by Sam King.

It was this result, perhaps, that led *Daily Telegraph* golf writer Leonard Crawley to suggest that another Alliss, myself, ought to play in the 1949 match at Ganton. He felt that we had no real chance and that I, as the best emerging talent, might as well be blooded.

I was just eighteen, with no record of tournament success behind me. It's not surprising that his advice went unheeded, though I suppose it was my first connection with the Ryder Cup. We did far better than expected and might well have won, eventually losing by 7 points to 5. We'd led by 3 to 1 after the first day's foursomes, and the margin was the same after the first four singles. Alas, our last four players all lost. Consequently we no longer thought the Americans quite as invincible, even though we were thrashed 9½ to 2½ in 1951. When they next came over in 1953 hopes were high, and there was much talk of a new 'Elizabethan

Age'. A queen had been crowned, Everest climbed and the Ashes won. Many thought the Ryder Cup would return that autumn at Wentworth for the first time in twenty years.

I was consistently having good finishes in tournaments and was overjoyed to be picked for the team at the age of twenty-two, with Bernard Hunt, a year older, the two youngsters amongst the veterans.

Nerves atremble, I was put into the top match of the foursomes, partnered by that mighty hitter Harry Weetman, against Dale Douglas and Ed 'Porky' Oliver. However, nerves or not, I found I was in command of my game and the match was close all the way. Mainly as a result of two putts of indecent length from Oliver, the Americans came to the 35th hole, the 570-yard 17th so well known from TV today, two up. Then, glory be, they drove out of bounds. At worst, it looked as if a 5 would give us the hole and the match would go to the last all square. At this point Harry Weetman hit a very poor tee shot. The best you could say about it was that it was in bounds and straight – but was skied only about 150 yards. I followed with a 5-iron safely up the fairway and Harry was left with a longish pitch to the green, which he thinned through. The Americans then put their fifth shot about three yards from the hole and I pitched up to about four feet. They got theirs and Harry missed. It was all over by 2 and 1.

Despite those high hopes, the first day continued to go badly for our team. The Irishmen Fred Daly and Harry Bradshaw beat Walter Burkemo and Cary Middlecoff by one hole, but in between there were two heavy defeats for Great Britain, Eric Brown and John Penton losing 8 and 7 and Jimmy Adams and Bernard Hunt by 7 and 5. How often it had been said that we started off with an in-built advantage because of our supposed greater experience at foursomes play. True, American professionals play no foursomes at all to my knowledge, but we ourselves play very little. Sadly, foursomes are a treasured feature of golf at only a few clubs these days.

Our captain, Henry Cotton, told me that I should have little difficulty in my singles the following day. He considered my opponent, Jim Turnesa, the weakest player on their team and the US captain, Lloyd Mangrum, hadn't picked him for the foursomes, which may have meant he had the same opinion.

At 3 to 1 down we certainly needed a fast start in the eight singles to get ourselves back into the match, and this we got from Fred Daly who, playing second, thrashed Ted Kroll 9 and 7. However, Dai Rees lost his match, but this was balanced by Eric Brown beating the formidable Mangrum two up. The score stood at 4 to 3 to the Americans.

Then came a miracle. Undoubtedly Snead was the most feared of our opponents, and with six holes to play stood four up on Harry Weetman. Unbelievably he then launched into a sequence of wild shots. Harry played steadily, but was more or less handed the match one up. The scores stood at USA 5, Great Britain 4, after Max Faulkner had lost to Middlecoff 3 and 2.

Meanwhile, Jim Turnesa had not been proving a weak link in the US team by any means. I was round in 70, which was then four under par, yet still went into lunch one down. However, I came to the 16th tee in the afternoon one up, and was further encouraged when Turnesa sliced wildly towards the woods. Surely he'd finish out of bounds? Alas, no. His ball struck a woman spectator and left him in play. However, he put his second shot into a bunker short of the green.

My own second shot was straight at the flag but struck a little heavily. I always knew it would be short, and so it was, in the front bunker forty yards from the hole. Turnesa then recovered to about ten feet, and my own third shot pulled up about five feet from the hole. He holed his putt. I missed. All square with two to play and the Ryder Cup in the balance, especially as I knew Harry Bradshaw had beaten Fred Haas. It was up to the youngsters, Alliss and Bernard Hunt, to bring the Cup back.

Turnesa drove off safely. My own plan was to hug the out of bounds along the left, then just ten yards off the fairway with my drive and let my normal fade bring the ball back to the middle of the fairway. Some might think it a risky shot but my driving had this consistent pattern. Alas, the fade didn't take and my straight shot was out of bounds by no more than a couple of feet.

At one down with one to play I could no longer win my match (extra holes have never been played in the Ryder Cup). If, however, I could get a half and Bernard Hunt, playing just behind, could win his match we would get the Cup back for the first time in the twenty years, since my father had been in that 1933 winning team. The 18th is 500 yards long. If you drive to the centre or left of the fairway, a long iron will probably get you home in two. As you go right with your tee shot, a faded wooden club second is needed, swinging left to right around the trees. Turnesa, playing first, put his drive way right, some fifty yards into the trees, surely lost or unplayable. I followed with a shot to the perfect position. After much deliberation and with a little luck, Turnesa got his out of the trees and then hit his third shot to some thirty yards short of the green. My second shot with a 2-iron was well struck but pulled a little, about fifteen yards off the green and thirty yards from the flag. Turnesa then pitched up to about five yards.

Many thoughts ran through my mind. For instance, I felt I had to reckon on the American holing out for a 5. I wanted to play a little run-up with my 9-iron up the slope from the small grassy, rather soggy, hollow where my ball lay. That way I'd be sure of my 5, but the run of the ball would be unpredictable. Even a perfect shot could finish ten feet away.

Needing a 4 I decided to pitch with my sand wedge, but negative thoughts were washing into my mind. I caught the ground behind the ball and left it short on the bank of the green. It was still my turn. This time I chipped with a 9-iron, running the ball up to about forty inches.

34

Turnesa followed by doing the decent thing – he missed. I had this little putt to win the hole and get a half out of my match and leave the Ryder Cup in the balance. I never touched the hole.

It was all made worse fifteen minutes later when Bernard Hunt came to the last green needing to get down in two putts to win his match (which would have made the scores level), but he took three.

The cause of youth didn't benefit and, when Ryder Cup time came round in 1955, we weren't picked. Both Hunt and I were back in the team in 1957. Again hopes were high. After all, we should have won in 1953. Many thought that this was our strongest Ryder Cup team, while the Americans, without Snead, Hogan and Middle-coff, looked a less-menacing bunch than usual.

Even so, the foursomes, in which Americans are thought to be at a disadvantage, once more went decisively their way by 3 matches to 1, with Bernard Hunt and I, playing in the first match out, losing by 2 and 1 to Doug Ford and Dow Finsterwald.

Our captain, Dai Rees, was not dismayed and went round his team saying how the singles draw had worked out very well for our side. In my case, he said, I'd have no trouble at all in disposing of Fred Hawkins, 'the weakest man on their team'. Max Faulkner asked to be dropped from the singles as he was playing badly, but Harry Weetman was furious to be left out. With certain tempers flaring, it didn't augur well for the morrow.

Yet 5 October 1957 at Lindrick was to be an amazing day. The iron men of America first faltered, then cracked, and finally collapsed altogether. After the first eighteen holes almost all of our men were up, and in the afternoon the cheering was particularly loud from around the turn as American after American went down, often by almost unbelievable margins. Dai Rees and Christy O'Connor both won 7 and 6, Bernard Hunt by 6 and 5, Peter Mills 5 and 3 and both Eric Brown and Ken Bousfield 4 and 3. The crowds were running wild, sensing victory.

Meanwhile, I was having a stern battle with Fred Hawkins and was one up at lunch, having gone round in 70. In the afternoon, at the 13th, then a par-5 of 470 yards, I looked likely to go further ahead until Hawkins holed a long putt for a half in 4 and then birdied the next to draw level. At the 16th, 486 yards, he went ahead with another birdie but then faltered at the 17th, a par-4 of 387 yards, when he was short in two. As I prepared to play my own shot to the green, Rees and Ken Bousfield came up. 'It doesn't matter,' Dai said, 'we've won, we've won, relax, we've won!'

Of course, I was highly delighted, but the news did nothing for my concentration and I sent my second shot under a hedge to the right of the green. I could do no better than 6 and Hawkins had only to make a 5 to win the hole and the match 2 and 1. Although I was playing number three, only Harry Bradshaw, having a very close match with US Open Champion Dick Mayer, and I were still out on the course. Harry halved his match in fine style.

The Ryder Cup was back in Britain for the first time in twenty-four years, but my own matchplay record read played four, lost four. Nevertheless, I was very proud to be a member of the winning team, and the memory has been warm and bright over the many years that were to pass before we found the men who could do it again.

Although I hadn't won a point, I felt that I had played as well as anyone in the team: in matchplay how your opponent plays is every bit as important. Even so, matchplay seemed to be a problem for me as it was for Seve Ballesteros in his early years. You can play well but your opponent, perhaps thought to have little chance, raises his game and has all the luck at vital moments.

The 1959 Ryder Cup in California went as many had feared. On home ground the Americans returned to their invincible ways. We won only two points, but in this match at the New Eldorado Club in Palm Desert I really arrived as a Ryder Cup player and began a long, wonderful partnership with Christy O'Connor. With him I won my first point when we beat Doug Ford and Art Wall in the foursomes 3 and 2. In the singles I halved my match with Jay Hebert, who went on to win the US PGA Championship the following year. It was a close contest the whole way, and I came to the last hole one down. Hebert found water with his second shot, thank the Lord, and I managed to put a straight 3-iron plumb in the middle of the green and won the hole.

1961 saw great changes in how the Ryder Cup was played. The four foursomes and eight singles, each of thirty-six holes were scrapped. Instead, all matches switched to eighteen holes, with two lots of four foursomes on the first day and eight singles, morning and afternoon.

Again we began badly in the foursomes, almost putting ourselves out of the contest on the first day, by the close of which the Americans led 6 matches to 2. O'Connor and I had started the match off well enough, however, by beating Gene Littler and Doug Ford 4 and 3. Even so, the second day has resulted in some of my most vivid Ryder Cup memories.

I was drawn to meet Palmer in the morning, a daunting prospect indeed at the time. He was at his very peak, and his famous charges against all the odds had already become legendary. He'd won the Masters twice, the US Open and our own Open a little over two months before at Royal Birkdale. There his performance had included some of the greatest golf ever seen in gale-force winds.

One of his greatest strengths was bold putting. He went firmly for everything, confident that if he ran a few feet past, he could still will the return putt in. Of course he did miss a few, but this went generally unnoticed. Perhaps he was a little like Tom Watson in his prime, never short, fully prepared to straighten out a borrow by hitting firmly at the back of the hole. His long game won him even more fans. He set himself to give the ball the biggest crack he could manage. Away the ball fizzed, and the fact that Arnold almost always finished off balance only increased the feeling of power.

I was pleased to find myself in a match that was the morning's main attraction, nervous, but in a positive way. I was playing well and didn't believe there was anyone in the world who could make me look silly on a golf course. I felt he'd have to play well to beat me and it wouldn't be 6 and 5 for sure.

Even though that match is quarter of a century ago, I can still remember every shot. This is how it went.

The 1st at Royal Lytham is a tester, a par-3 of just over 200 yards. After a half in 3s, Palmer went one up when we were both short of the 2nd in two and he succeeded in getting down with a chip and a putt. However, I was immediately able to come back at him with two wins, the second as the result of a wedge to a couple of feet or so at the 4th. The next two holes were halved. Then we faced the 7th, a long par-5 of 550 yards, unreachable that day into a stiff wind. Just off the green with my third shot, I chipped stone dead. Palmer was a few feet on to the back fringe in three. Out came his putter; his ball raced at the hole much too hard, I thought, but no, bang! it hit the hole and plunged in. Match all square – blast him!

However, from through the green at the 8th he was less successful, not hitting his chip clean and I went one up again. I was lucky to get a half at the 9th, 162 yards, where Arnold hit the middle of the green, and I bunkered my 7-iron on the right but got down in two more, holing a very missable putt.

At the 10th, 334 yards, I looked about to go further ahead when I hit my little pitch to about a yard while he pitched through the green into ankle-deep rough. I thought he had no chance of stopping his chip anywhere near the hole. Instead, he holed it. Blast him again!

The next four holes were halved, and at the par-5 15th we both drove well. My second shot ended just a few feet short of the green, but Arnold had hooked into a bunker. I chipped close, only two or three feet away. Palmer then played his bunker shot much too hard. It flew out, bounced once and then went straight into the hole on the fly. Well, I thought, this is the kind of crash, bang play I expected from him. Match all square again. Blast him for the third time!

On the next two holes we both had chances, but they were halved in par. Palmer had the honour on the last, a par-4 of 380 or so yards downwind. He smashed his drive away into the far distance and, though I carried the bunkers on the left, my ball settled in the semi-rough, on a tuft a couple of inches off the ground. Afraid of getting a flier, I decided to hit at it as hard as I could with my wedge but got underneath the ball, finishing just short of the green. Palmer played a good pitch, six yards short of the hole.

Damn it, I felt I'd had the edge from the 3rd hole and, but for those three shots holed from off the green . . . Now it looked as if I was going to lose. There he was, just a few yards away and I had some forty yards to the hole. Well, I hated the thought of losing the match to a par on the last hole and steeled myself to get the chip as close as I could.

I took out my 9-iron, the club I trusted most for a running shot, got my hands well forward and struck the ball with exactly the strength and precision I wanted. On and on it went and then, for just a moment, I thought, it's going in! In fact, it caught the edge of the hole and finished less than a couple of feet past.

Palmer settled into his knock-kneed putting stance. The stroke was firm and I held my breath as his ball ran at the hole. No, it wasn't in and stopped a missable distance past, about two-and-a-half feet or so.

I walked up to my putt. 'Pick it up,' Palmer said. Impassively I did so, but I was much relieved. Palmer was looking a little cross. Perhaps he'd expected to hole his first putt and I'm sure he must have expected to win the match. Now he had the two-and-a-half footer to half it.

Unbidden, the words tumbled out: 'That's all right,' I said, 'pick it up Arnold.'

It was the most memorable match of my career as a

Ryder Cup player. However, two years later came another Alliss versus Palmer Ryder Cup match at Bobby Jones's boyhood course, East Lake, Atlanta, Georgia and my memories of it are nearly as sharp. I was in poor driving form, no width and too much lift on the back swing, followed by a chop across the ball. I was hitting my tee shots little more than 220 yards. Palmer was lacing his about fifty yards past me every time. But this needn't always be a disadvantage if the irons are going well. Mine were, and I was usually inside his shots to the greens on the early holes. In fact, I should have opened up a gap of perhaps three holes, but missed three putts of five feet or less. At the 9th, a par-5 of just over 500 yards, I got a good one away at last and found the green with my second to win it with a 4. I won the 12th as well, holing a putt of three or four yards. I soon lost one of my two-hole lead when I missed a short putt on the 14th, but Palmer was immediately kind to me on the 15th, a par-5. He hooked his tee shot and bunkered his second so I won it with a par: two up with three to play.

Par golf should have done it, but I then promptly dropped a shot when I missed the green at the 15th and lost the hole. The match seemed more or less mine, however, when I struck a 6-iron twelve-feet from the hole at the 410-yard 17th. But Palmer's approach was much better, only a yard away. It was odds on the match going to the last all square. This time my putting worked well. I got mine in to the loudest silence I've ever heard! Palmer had to hole his to stay in the match.

He did, and strode eagerly to the last, a 230-yard par-3. Here he fired his tee shot straight at the flag, but was long by several yards. Nevertheless, it looked a certain par. The first job was to get my ball on the green. This I did, but cut it a little, finishing some twenty yards from the hole with a huge borrow from the right. My putt was one of the best long ones of my entire competitive career, and struck at a moment when it really counted. On and on it rolled, pace and judgement of line always looking good. I began to wonder if it would die into the hole.

Well, it nearly did, stopping just inches away. Palmer knocked my ball towards me. He had to hole for a birdie 2 to halve the match.

I was expecting that very bold putter at least to give me a bit of a fright with his putt, to threaten the hole. That he did, but much too hard. I had beaten the hero on his own ground.

Although my memories up to 1963 have mostly been of my singles matches, my best overall Ryder Cup golf was played at Royal Birkdale in 1965, when the O'Connor and Alliss pairing worked very well indeed. In the morning's foursomes we weren't stretched by Don January and Ken Venturi. One under par when the match ended, we won by a very convincing margin of 5 and 4. In the afternoon we shifted up a gear, going to the turn in thirty-one strokes, but were only one up against Billy Casper and Gene Littler. We kept on playing sub-par golf, however, and came through in the end by 2 and 1.

After that first day both teams were level at 4–4 and Christy O'Connor and I were brimming with confidence on the second morning, facing Dave Marr, that year's US PGA Champion, and, yes, Arnold Palmer. In the event, we played approximate par golf and that isn't often good enough in fourball play. We went down 5 and 4, and after a hurried lunch, were first off in the afternoon, much less confident this time, especially as the luck of the draw had us out against Marr and Palmer again. However, the match was evenly balanced all the way, and we came to the last at Royal Birkdale, a par-5 in those days, all square. Both pairs were several strokes under par. That day the 513 yards really needed two good shots with a driver to get home in two. My first was a good one, down the right half of the fairway. O'Connor was bunkered, Marr hit a short tee shot and Palmer was in trouble on the right. I was not happy at the thought of having to go with my driver as the lie was tight. A number 4 was the only other wooden club I had in my bag. I decided to play the shot with my hands a little further ahead of the ball than usual and with the club

41

toed in a little, a tip from John Jacobs. Now could I swing freely? It was as sweet a shot as I ever hit. Away it flew on line with the right edge of the green. Then a little draw began to take. My ball turned towards the flag, took one big bounce and rolled on, stopping no more than four yards from the hole.

Neither Dave Marr nor Arnold Palmer could do anything about it, and in the end they didn't even ask me to putt. Christy and I shook hands, winners one up. Despite this victory the score was Great Britain and Ireland 6; USA 8 at the end of the second day's play. There were two groups of eight singles left to play so the match was by no means over.

This isn't a blow-by-blow history of the Ryder Cup but just my clearest memories of it, so I won't go too far into the painful details of the third and last day's play. It was very nearly a rout, for the result was hardly in doubt after our first four players all lost in the morning. Overall, the Americans won the singles by 10 points to 5.

It was a good day for me because I beat two US Open Champions, Billy Casper, who is now a considerable force on the US Senior Tour, and Ken Venturi, now a TV golf commentator in the USA. In the morning I went to the turn in 32 against Casper's 33, and the inward nine was equally closely contested. I had a putt of some five feet for the match on the final green – not my best distance – but I banged it in, much to the crowd's and my delight.

In the afternoon I found Ken Venturi a steady opponent, especially over the first nine, but I was able to pull away later, winning 3 and 1.

With 5 points from my six matches I had enjoyed my best Ryder Cup, being involved in nearly half of our points total. One reward was my only invitation to play in the World Matchplay Championship at Wentworth.

There were a few more great days for Peter Alliss in the Ryder Cup. In 1967, however, I vividly remember we all felt one down before any of us so much as reached the first tee. At the pre-Ryder Cup dinner, Dai Rees, called to the colours once again as captain, introduced his team one by one, singling out our 'greatest' achievements. In some cases these were really rather slim. To be honest, it was a little embarrassing. Ben Hogan, captaining the USA, topped Dai's remarks very effectively, asking his team to rise to their feet and then saying: 'Ladies and gentlemen, simply the finest golfers in the world.' What an introduction!

We went on to lose 21–6, and the team of O'Connor and Alliss were eclipsed in both the foursomes and fourballs. In the singles I lost a close match to Billy Casper 2 and 1, but beat Gay Brewer, US Masters Champion that year, 2 and 1. Hogan's statement had become hard fact.

When Ryder Cup time came round again in 1969, memories of our Lindrick triumph twelve years before were growing dim. The Americans had certainly re-established their supremacy on both sides of the Atlantic in the years that followed. However, in Eric Brown we had a very competitive captain, so much so that he forbade us looking for US balls in the rough in case we incurred a penalty stroke by treading on one and moving it.

Our team was very much a mixture of young players and long-established warriors, with O'Connor, Bernard Hunt and I having the most years of Ryder Cup experience. The key figures of our team were to be Tony Jacklin, our recent Open Champion and Peter Townsend, at that time equally the coming man of British golf.

The first morning saw hardly a breath of wind, conditions that surely favoured the American team. But no, there was a euphoric start as our foursomes pairings of Coles/Huggett, Gallacher/Bembridge and Jacklin/Townsend all won without needing to play the 18th. I saw none of this, being involved with Christy O'Connor in hard battle with Billy Casper and Frank Beard, two prolific money-winners on the US Tour.

With a birdie at the 1st we jumped straight into the lead, but then lost both the 3rd and 4th holes to pars to go one down. We then had birdies at the 6th and 7th to take the lead. The match was all square at the turn. At the 13th, then 517 yards, an American birdie put us behind but we immediately squared with a 2 on the 202-yard 14th. The remaining holes were all halved, though I had a putt of about eighteen feet to win the match at the last. I thought I had it, but the ball flicked around the rim and that was that.

In the afternoon I was an observer, commentating with Henry Longhurst and Harry Carpenter for the BBC. It did not go well. Sam Snead, the American captain, having used ripe language on his team at lunch, had his men raring to go. Our first two foursomes pairings both lost close matches, but Tony Jacklin and Peter Townsend then birdied the last two holes to beat Billy Casper and Frank Beard one up.

In the final foursome Jack Nicklaus made his first Ryder Cup appearance no fewer than seven years after he had won his first major professional championship, the 1962 US Open. (Yes, there've been many arguments over first the British and later the European selection procedures for the Ryder Cup. The American notion that you had to serve out a number of years as a member of the US Professional Golfers' Association before becoming eligible was just as controversial as anything contrived by committees this side of the Atlantic! Only after the near defeat of 1983 in Florida were they to produce a more logical system, though still not ideal.)

This final match, between Nicklaus and Dan Sikes and Bernard Hunt and Peter Butler, produced nothing in the way of scoring but plenty of excitement. With the match all square on the 510-yard 17th, both pairs took 6 and Nicklaus then hooked his tee shot into the rough on the last hole. Minutes later, however, he played a match-winning shot to this par-5 when he wedged the Americans' third shot to a couple of feet, leaving Bernard Hunt with a long putt to halve the hole in 4s. It missed.

The day ended with Great Britain having a 1-point lead, but some of the momentum was gone. Even so,

Great Britain proved to have the better morning golfers on the second day when the two sets of fourballs began. Eric Brown made the possibly risky decision to split the successful pairing of Peter Townsend and Tony Jacklin to 'spread the inspiration around'. One result was that I'd played my last match with Christy O'Connor. He went out first with Townsend and won, while the new combination of Jacklin and Neil Coles playing at number four beat Nicklaus and Sikes. In between, Brian Huggett and Alex Caygill (the latter an outstanding talent but who sadly proved far less successful at controlling his life) halved their match with Ray Floyd and Miller Barber.

My new partner was Brian Barnes. We faced Lee Trevino and Gene Littler, a rather idiosyncratic American pairing. Trevino 'looks wrong' but is perfect through the ball, while Littler is perfect in everything he does except that his tournament results, despite one US Amateur Championship and one US Open, are well below what his genius for the game might have achieved.

Brian and I were one under par over the first seven holes and three down, but birdies on the 9th and 10th brought us back into the match. On the 15th we got the match back to all square, but Trevino holed a long putt at the 17th to take the Americans into the lead once again. Both sides birdied the last, so Barnes and Alliss, though six under par at the finish, lost by one hole.

Overall, however, the match was looking good for the home team. We went into the afternoon series of fourballs with a 2-point lead.

In the first match Peter Townsend and Peter Butler were five under par at the finish, but that wasn't good enough to beat Billy Casper and Frank Beard, who won by two up. There followed the most ill-tempered match in the history of the Ryder Cup. It was between Brian Huggett and Bernard Gallacher and Dave Hill and Ken Still.

All was peace until the match reached the 7th green, with the American pair two up. Here, Dave Hill putted out of turn and Huggett mentioned this to the match referee. Under the rules of golf Hill could have replaced his ball and waited his turn, but Ken Still swept towards the 8th tee declaring: 'If you want to win that badly, you can have the hole.'

As the match went down the 8th fairway, Huggett and Still exchanged unfriendly words and the crowd became aware of the ill feeling. There was a little booing and one spectator was restrained from throwing a bottle.

It was definitely time for a pause to let the heart beats slow down. Unfortunately, events on the 8th green quickened them even more. Ken Still, with a putt for a birdie, charged it past the hole and then prepared to putt out, intent on giving his partner, Dave Hill, a 'free putt' from about four feet. Bernard Gallacher, thinking that the borrow of Still's second putt might give his American partner a little useful information, picked up Still's ball and tossed it to him , conceding the par-4. Still was very cross and claimed that Great Britain had conceded the hole because his own ball had been touched. An international incident was in the making, perhaps inflamed when Dave Hill holed his short putt for a birdie and bowed ironically to the crowd. Officials from both the British and US PGA began to move towards the trouble spot to have a word here and there to the effect that it was really just a game – wasn't it?

A few holes later, two policemen arrived on the scene, followed by a few of the US team to urge and counsel their men.

There were no more incidents, and despite the clamour the golf remained of a high standard, typified by Dave Hill hitting the 510-yard 17th green in two and then holing his putt for an eagle 3 and a 2 and 1 victory. 'That'll teach 'em,' he seemed to be saying.

All in all, I suppose this match saw the most heated tempers in the whole long Ryder Cup saga. Even so, it amounted to little more than a cross word or two and even added spice to the occasion. After all, matchplay, rare as it is, does inflame the passions more than a run-of-the-mill seventy-two holes strokeplay tournament. It's about *us* beating *them*, whichever team you happen to support, and if *they* get into deep rough or a bunker spectators are likely to rejoice. In strokeplay, all of us think far more about how the players are faring. There will be applause after a good shot and a sympathetic groan when a player's ball plummets down into trouble.

When the last two matches were halved, the USA had pulled back two points that afternoon and the two sides were level, each having won six matches with three halved.

I remember our team was a little disappointed. We had lost our good lead from the first morning's play, and I felt the greater American strength in depth might tell over the final sixteen singles matches. It was a moment-ous day for me on a personal level. I had decided to give up international team golf, so this was my final match. I had a great opponent, Lee Trevino, US Open Champion the previous year but not yet quite the name he was to become over the next few years.

Playing at number one I had a great start, with birdies on the first two holes to go two up. The next four holes were halved in par figures, but Trevino then birdied three of the next four holes to be up in the match for the first time at the 10th. The next five holes were all halved with pars, but I faltered at the 16th, 401 yards, dropping a shot to be two down with two to play. At this point I got my third birdie of the morning on this 510-yard hole but, alas for Alliss, so did Trevino, running out the winner 2 and 1. I had only dropped that one shot to par in my round and was two under at the finish, but Trevino produced the best scoring to be five under. I had missed eight putts of under ten feet and that, I thought, was enough of that.

My defeat was a jolt to our team hopes, and matters became worse when our number two, Peter Townsend, went down 5 and 4 to Dave Hill.

Could Neil Coles deal with Tommy Aaron, one of the Americans not on good form? He was in the lead at the turn by one hole, and then took the 10th as well. Neil then ran into trouble, losing three holes in a row to be down in the match for the first time and holes running out. The 14th and 15th were halved, but Coles then levelled the match when he holed a good putt on the 16th. Even better was to follow. On the par-5 17th, Coles drove well and then got his 4-wood shot to within inches of the hole. He was one up again and went on to take the match. The rot seemed to have stopped. Christy O'Connor defeated Frank Beard far from home 5 and 4, but Brian Barnes lost a close match to Billy Casper by one hole.

At this point the Great Britain tail wagged vigorously. Maurice Bembridge and Peter Butler each won one up. On to the last match, which featured our Open Champion Tony Jacklin and Jack Nicklaus. It drew the biggest crowds, and Jacklin put on a fine show, victoriously coasting in 4 and 3.

Once again Great Britain had had the better of a morning's play and regained a 2-point lead. Three wins and a half in the afternoon's eight singles would bring the Ryder Cup home.

The play which followed is best remembered for the tremendous climax. The strain by now was telling on all the players, and you could hardly say that more than three players produced good figures. At number one and three both Brian Barnes and Maurice Bembridge played downright badly and beat themselves, but Bernard Gallacher, replacing Peter Townsend or me, went some way towards redressing the balance. He was four under par when he beat Trevino 4 and 3. That was one of the 3½ points.

Peter Butler seemed to be bringing in another with ease when he was three up on Dale Douglass after four holes. The American fought back, however, to level the match after the 10th. But Peter Butler was a very steely competitor and continued undisturbed to a 3 and 2 victory. Only a win and a half were needed from the last four matches. The signs were good, for we had won them all in the morning.

It was a very different story this time. O'Connor was below his best against Gene Littler and lost 2 and 1. Neil Coles was not himself and was five over par when he lost 4 and 3 to Dan Sikes. Suddenly those 1½ points had to come from just two matches, Brian Huggett against Billy Casper and Tony Jacklin against Jack Nicklaus.

The Huggett/Casper match was square at the turn, but the American took a one-hole lead when Huggett dropped a shot at the 10th. Five halves followed, but then Casper was twice bunkered at the 16th and had to concede the hole. Match all square.

The last two holes at Royal Birkdale measured 510 and 513 yards, but both were clear birdie opportunities. On the 17th Casper chipped dead for his and left Huggett facing a putt of four feet or so to get his half. This he bravely did.

On the last, both Casper and Huggett reached the green in two. With a thirty-foot putt to win the match Huggett went boldly at it; rather too boldly in fact. He ran the ball a little more than four feet past, and shortly after heard a roar from the crowd at the 17th green. To Huggett this meant that Jacklin had won his match with Nicklaus, and that he had to hole the four-footer for a half to win the Ryder Cup. He did so and collapsed in a mixture of relief and triumph. But all was not over, as he had thought.

Behind, Jacklin and Nicklaus had been having a tremendous battle, the lead, ever changing hands, first one player then the other being pulled back to all square and never more than one hole in it. At the 16th, however, Jacklin dropped a shot to go one down, and on the 17th Nicklaus had the best of things when he put his iron shot about eighteen feet from the flag with Jacklin as many yards away. Jacklin holed his huge putt, the reason for that great roar from the crowd. Nicklaus didn't. Match all square.

So the Ryder Cup hadn't been won after all; the outcome of the match now depended on how the two men played just one hole, ironic after the hundreds played over the three days. Either man could win or lose the Cup.

Both drove well and Nicklaus was first to play to the green, a good one, his ball ending about half a dozen yards from the flag. Jacklin's ball flew straight on target but ran past to the back of the green, a great deal further away. He had a putt probably to win the Ryder Cup while to three-putt made the reverse inevitable. His ball ran on line, but pulled up about two-and-a-half feet short. It was Nicklaus's turn to try to take the trophy. He was determined not to be short. Nor was he. He had to hole the one back from about four feet or the Cup would go to Great Britain.

Though Nicklaus is not one of the world's greatest putters, he's the man I'd always choose to get in a vital putt. As he says: 'You have to bear down on them. Any jerk can miss them gracefully.'

Nicklaus did hole and quickly said to Jacklin: 'I don't think you would have missed but in these circumstances I would never give you the opportunity.' The gesture set the seal on this great occasion and removed all trace of the ill feeling that had broken out in the fourball matches. Even so, Jacklin said afterwards: 'Half of his team were bitching about the fact he gave me that putt.'

At a far more vital moment, it somehow echoed my own gesture with Palmer at Lytham eight years before and was a fitting end to my own Ryder Cup career. I had watched for more than half the match from the commentary box. That was to be my viewpoint always in the years that lay ahead and what great years they were. The 1983 match in America was almost as tense as this Jacklin/Nicklaus finale and then, of course, came the triumph at The Belfry in 1985.

5

Triumph and Tragedy

Bob Charles had the honour at the 18th tee on the final hole of the 1969 Open Championship. He pulled his drive to the right, turned to his caddie and said, 'It's in the trap.' Tony Jacklin thought he knew better. He was sure he'd seen Charles's ball skip past the bunker into some light rough.

It made a difference. The New Zealander shouldn't have much difficulty in hitting the green from there. If he one-putted for a birdie, and Tony took 5, his two-stroke lead would be gone and the championship would be decided the following day over an eighteenth-hole play-off.

The 389-yard final hole at Royal Lytham and St Anne's is a good one. Many have come to grief there over the years, usually through bunkering their tee shot and so being unable to reach the green in two. Charles had put the negative thought of the bunkers into Tony's mind, but he quickly told himself to make a good swing.

Body obeyed mind and, as commentator Henry Long-hurst said on TV: 'What a corker'. It was dead straight and just about the longest seen on the hole all week. Jacklin had 140 yards to the flag and debated his shot, while Charles played to the green about twenty feet from the hole. Knowing when the adrenalin is flowing he might hit an unwanted extra twenty yards, Tony decided on a three-quarter shot with his favourite 7-iron. His ball came to rest about fifteen feet from the flag and, when Charles had missed his birdie putt, he took two putts to win the title by two strokes.

He was the first home-grown champion since 1951. Fame and fortune were his. In later years, however, Jacklin came to think that the 1969 Open was not one of his best performances. He had relied a little too heavily on his putting and recovery play from bunkers. It had been a flawed performance as regards quality of play from tee to green. On the final day he had done nothing startling, just a steady round of 72, one over par, and none of the other contenders had made a run at his two-stroke lead. Of the next six high finishers only one was better than 72, and you had to look down to eighth place before finding a brilliant score, a 66 from Peter Alliss. Alas, I had started the day twelve strokes behind . . .

At this time Jacklin had been playing on the US Tour. He wanted the stiffest competition to temper his game and also the prize money was far, far higher than anything in Europe. In America he had made a name for himself by his success in the 1968 Jacksonville Open, the first British player to win a full US Tour event since Ted Ray, back in 1920.

In 1970 he showed good form once more, with several high finishes, which included a tie for the San Diego Open before losing in a play-off to Pete Brown and a second place in the Tournament of Champions. On 18 June 1970 he stepped onto the 1st tee at Hazeltine Country Club, Chaska, Minnesota in good heart. However, he wasn't expecting to win the US Open for he had missed the halfway cut the previous week, putting very badly indeed.

But for Jacklin the weather felt just like home in Scunthorpe, Lincolnshire. It was cold, with the winds gusting to 40 m.p.h. He could cope with all that and knew many wouldn't relish the conditions. Arnold Palmer took 79 that first day, Gary Player 80 and Nicklaus a hardly credible 81. Trevino, an excellent wind player, was little better. His 77 meant that he too was not likely to feature at the finish.

Jacklin had the start he wanted, a fifteen-foot putt on the 1st for a birdie. On the 2nd he hooked his tee shot into bushes, but managed to find a tiny gap for his second shot. After six holes he was three under par and on the march. He reached the turn in 33, and then holed a bunker shot on the 12th and birdied the 15th. As he reached the 17th tee, he was running away with the championship. It was a short par-4 of just 344 yards but Jacklin faltered, hitting his approach shot into water and ending up with a 6 on his card. He finished his round with a 71, one under par. It wasn't a startling score, but it was two better than the next man, Julius Boros.

What had happened? Apart from the weather, many were blaming the course. Nicklaus was polite enough, commenting that Hazeltine was as difficult as any used for a US Open. Dave Hill, rather an eccentric, let his opinions ring out. He declared the course should be ploughed up and given over to corn and perhaps a few cows. It was just pasture land with flags.

It's mostly thought you should approach a course with respect, even affection, if you want to do well on it. Dave Hill proved the exception – he hated it. But he played well, even though he was fined $150 for his rude comments – a bargain Hill thought. On the second day he moved into second place with a round of 69; Jacklin took 70. A pattern was becoming clear. If Jacklin dropped a shot, he came straight back with a birdie. If he missed a green, he got down in two. He had also found a formula for putting, a gimmick that worked that week. Simply get set, aim, look at the hole and fire. Trying it out on the putting green, he found that his striking and feel improved dramatically. The gimmick worked wonders and Jacklin was infallible from four to six feet and getting far more than his share of longer putts. He was averaging 28 per round. At the end of the day he was halfway to the championship and leading Hill by three strokes.

Despite improved weather conditions, Hazeltine continued to cause the players trouble. There were a variety of reasons. The par-5s, for instance, were not reachable in two, and ten of the fourteen driving holes were doglegs. It meant, as Nicklaus put it, 'There are no position Bs on the tee shots.' Surprisingly, for a course only some eight years old it was a little old-fashioned, having a large number of elevated greens. This meant the bottoms of the flags were not visible and, with vast greens, players were frequently a club or two out with their judgement of distance.

For the third round Jacklin was paired with Dave Hill, perhaps a stroke of good fortune. Normally he could have expected the crowds would have been behind an American golfer, but it was not so in this case. Minnesotans were displeased by Hill's criticism of the course and his suggestion that it was more suited to cows. They mooed as he played. Jacklin played a very steady round of 70 which contained one spectacular shot. On the 17th tee he hooked a 2-iron behind some trees. He then had about 160 yards to go with a tree to carry. He had to get the ball up quickly, but he also needed length. His shot had to be hit flat out. It came off. Jacklin cleared the tree and water beyond, reached the green and got his par. His 70 made this the position:

Jacklin	211
Hill	215
Gay Brewer	218

Only two other players were less than eleven strokes behind. Barring a series of disasters – and they have been known – only Dave Hill was still credibly within reach.

Waiting and hoping to play well after the noon hour when you're the championship leader is always hard on the nerves. We all want to be off, to get the first few holes over. Jacklin was no exception. But through the night he had great support from his wife. The Jacklin's seven-month-old son, Bradley, was teething and very unhappy. Vivien took both son and herself off to the bathroom for the night so her man might sleep – if sleep he could – undisturbed. It's a little like the tale of Jack Nicklaus and his wife Barbara at the 1978 Open Championship. Jack thought the double bed too narrow for both of them and surely he had to 'protect the property'. Barbara made do with a camp bed.

The waiting was at last over. Jacklin began his final round steadily enough. After six holes he was one under par for the round, and then on the 7th rasped a 4-iron over the water to some four feet. If he got that putt, he'd be miles ahead. Although this was the length Jacklin had been infallible at all week, he missed – but it was still a par. On the next, Jacklin cracked a 2-iron at the flag but too long, finishing about thirty feet past. Cautiously he left his first putt about five feet short and missed that also. Doubts began to wash in. At the 9th he pulled his tee shot into the rough, but succeeded in getting his next shot onto the green – but another thirty-footer had to be faced. Having been short just before, Jacklin overcompensated or, some thought, gave his ball a tense stab. It raced at the hole, far too strong, but the line could hardly have been improved on. His ball hit the back of the hole, hopped high in the air and down to the bottom of the cup. A birdie, when he might have been ten feet, even more, past the hole.

It was a decisive shot. Jacklin himself thought it won him the championship. Although he was still level par after playing the 8th, the self-doubts had been intense. If he'd three-putted the 9th as well, Jacklin, surprisingly I think, believes he would have lost the championship, even though no one else, as at Royal Lytham and St Anne's the year before, was making a real run at him.

He began to enjoy the experience, picked up two more birdies on the way home and came to the last with a six-stroke lead. He drove well and put a 6-iron on the green. Again he had a putt of around thirty feet and again he struck it too firmly – not that it mattered at this point. Again he holed out. He was the first British player to win the US Open since Ted Ray, almost forgotten in the mists of time. His seven-stroke victory over Dave Hill, who finished with a 73 to Jacklin's 70, was the biggest since the Cornish-born-and-bred Jim Barnes cruised in nine strokes ahead of Walter Hagen and Fred McLeod in

1921. He had also joined the select group of Barnes, Walter Hagen and Ben Hogan as players who had won the US Open after leading throughout and Harry Vardon, Ted Ray and Gary Player as overseas-based golfers to win the US Open. The world was before him and, until the 1970 Open Championship at St Andrews the following month, as the holder of both titles he had fair claim to call himself the Champion of the World!

It was said his business manager Mark McCormack arranged a far too hectic schedule. Jacklin raced hither and thither for exhibition matches, company days, endorsement business meetings, television – and, yes, a fairly full programme of tournament golf as well. The money poured in, mainly as a result of his Lytham win but Hazeltine helped as well. One major championship doesn't bring in a fortune unless the player has a saleable personality; two majors is something else, especially if they come close together. Tony, for a while, looked to have the makings of becoming a star at the level of Nicklaus, Palmer and Player.

Shortly after, he added to the growing legend by an outward nine holes of 29 in the first round of the Open at St Andrews. Surely this was the answer to those who alleged he was doing too much money-making and his golf must suffer. Then came a freak storm, the course went under water and Jacklin's round was halted while he was at his inspirational best. He had to come back to finish his round the next day. The magic was gone. Still, a 67 was a good score and he was still very much in contention going into the final round, with Jack Nicklaus and Doug Sanders two behind the leader, Lee Trevino. His 76 relegated him to fifth place, but even so he was only three strokes away from the Sanders/Nicklaus play-off after Doug had missed that most famous of all short putts to win the championship outright.

When the championship went to Royal Birkdale the following year, Tony had established a remarkable sequence in the event. From 1965 he'd been twenty-fifth, thirtieth, fifth, eighteenth, first and fifth. This year he felt

56

his iron play was poor throughout, but he still brought in rounds of 69, 70 and 71. He was third, two strokes behind Lee Trevino and one behind the Taiwanese golfer Lu Liang Huan.

Playing just the first half of the American season, Jacklin had his best year in 1972. He had five finishes of seventh or better, and one of these was a win, the Greater Jacksonville Open, which he won after a sudden death play-off which, I do believe, must have made him the only British player to win more than two events on the US Tour. (Sandy Lyle's record is a little obscure for his first successes were not official money events.)

He was desperately keen to win another Open Championship, feeling himself due for another major title. At Muirfield in 1972 Jacklin was to play what he considers his best golf in any of his Opens, including his two victories. Remember no one had made a run at him at either Royal Lytham or Hazeltine. They certainly did at Muirfield.

Jacklin opened with a round of 69, despite the discouragement of three-putting the 1st green. He also finished with three putts, but in between had five birdies and the rest pars. Peter Tupling led with a 68, but Jacklin led the people who mattered with his 69. Nicklaus had a 70 and Trevino, Gary Player and Doug Sanders all 71s.

On the second day he took 72, and at the end of play headed the leader board with Trevino, who was round in 70. A stroke away were Player, Nicklaus, with two major titles under his belt already that year, Doug Sanders, and Johnny Miller (who had a 66 which included a 2 on a par-5) and others who were not to feature in the story later.

Jacklin had shown his resilience. On the 13th, a par-3 of about 150 yards, he was bunkered with his tee shot. He left his attempted recovery in the sand, and then his third shot went over the green into another bunker. He took three more to get down for a 6. It was a disaster, but Tony made up some of the lost ground by being two under par for the last five holes.

His resilience was to be tested even more by Trevino the following day. Jacklin had played with the Mexican for part of the time at Royal Birkdale the previous year when Trevino's putter was charmed. Now he had to do it again, over thirty-six holes. As leaders, they were out together for the third round, with Jacklin's putter working well on the first nine, holing some good long putts. He also had an eagle on the 5th to Trevino's birdie 4. Jacklin reached the turn three under par, while Trevino was level and going unspectacularly about his business. It all began to change at the 14th when Lee holed a putt of half a dozen yards for a birdie, but gained no ground on Jacklin. A much longer one went down on the next for another, but again Jacklin kept level with a good putt of his own. On the short 16th, nearly 200 yards, Tony's tee shot found the green, but Trevino was in sand on a downslope towards the rear of the bunker. It was a difficult shot and Trevino 'drove' his attempted 'splash' shot. For a moment his ball headed for more trouble on the other side of the green, but then it clattered into the flag stick and collapsed into the hole. A 2 for Trevino, while Jacklin had to be content with a par-3. The 17th, a par-5 of about 525 yards, was easily within range of two shots on the day and both birdied the hole. On the last, 430 yards, Jacklin was not quite firm enough with his second shot and had a long putt which he left six feet short. Trevino was a little long and went through the green on to the fringe. He then chipped his ball into the hole for his fifth consecutive birdie. Jacklin holed out for par and a round of 67, to Trevino's record-equalling 66.

But Jacklin still felt full of confidence for the morrow. He had taken all the American could throw at him. True, he might have been at least a couple of shots in the lead, but only had one stroke to make up the next day. He felt Trevino had used up all the luck any mortal was entitled to. It would be his turn in the final round and his game was sharp. Hadn't he been inside Trevino time and again on the shots to the green?

The odds were strongly on the championship lying between these two. This was the position as the final round began:

Trevino   207
Jacklin   208
Sanders   211
Barnes   212
Nicklaus   213

As Trevino remarked to Jacklin on the 1st tee: 'Jack might catch one of us – but not both'. Neither feared Sanders or Barnes, but a Nicklaus round in the mid 60s was on. Never was there more incentive for Jack to go for everything, for he had the target of all four majors in one year still within reach. Surely he would be going for every flag and every putt.

Nicklaus did indeed produce one of the greatest final rounds I can remember. He went to the turn in a rousing 32, and then birdied both 10th and 11th. This was scoring of the same order as Jacklin's start at St Andrews two years before. Jacklin and Trevino, playing a couple of holes behind, had to listen to the roars and cheering as Nicklaus unleashed a succession of superb iron shots at the flag and succeeded in nailing the putts. It was some consolation for them that Nicklaus had to pause a while on the 11th green as the applause rang out when both Trevino and Jacklin eagled the 9th, Jacklin from short range, Trevino from half a dozen yards. They certainly needed those putts.

For a few minutes, Nicklaus's onslaught had put him into the championship lead. And on the 12th, he had yet another clear chance for a birdie when he stopped his pitch three yards from the hole. But he missed the putt. However, he came close again on the next two holes. The 17th was a clear birdie opportunity, even though probably out of range in two that day, so Jack had a 64 in his sights. Alas for Jack, it went a little wrong on the run-in. The first real error came at the 16th, when his tee shot to this 180-yard par-3 landed on the front of the green and

60

the contours shrugged it away into the rough. He could not get down in two more to save his par.

The 64 was gone. Could he birdie the 540-yard 17th? Jack immediately made this very unlikely by hooking his tee shot into deep rough. His chance of reaching in two was gone, and in the event he could do little more than play out to the fairway. The 65 was no longer in prospect, but Jack finished bravely with two pars for a round of 66. This was good enough to make Trevino or Jacklin need to finish in par or better to win.

A forgotten error soon did much to cost Jacklin the championship. After he had birdied the 14th he was in a three-way tie, and quickly followed up with an iron shot to little more than three feet on the next hole. He missed it, but proved as resilient as ever on the 16th where he bunkered his tee shot, splashed out to about six feet and sank the vital putt for a par. This man just wasn't going to crack.

He went to the 17th needing two pars to beat Nicklaus, and a birdie on one of the two remaining holes might well beat Trevino.

About to drive, Trevino's concentration was momentarily disturbed by a TV cameraman. When he did get his shot away, he found a deep bunker along the left-hand side and could only just play out. Jacklin, on the other hand, drove perfectly. The picture was beginning to change, and Trevino faced disaster when he hit his third shot with a fairway wood well short of the green and into deep rough. Jacklin, also with a 3-wood, could not reach the green but his placement was admirable – over to the left a little, in light semi-rough and away from the mound that protects the approach from the right of the fairway. It was Trevino to play, his fourth shot through the green and up the slight slope. If the American took 6 and Jacklin could pitch and single-putt, he would have a one-stroke lead over both the Americans on the final hole.

The weather had been fine all week and the green looked fast and burned. With the pin towards the back,

Jacklin decided to play a running shot with his wedge. To me, the shot always looked a good one, and although the 17th green was hard it seemed to check unexpectedly and pulled up a little over five yards short of the hole.

Trevino to play, a man now thinking of second place, furious with himself for having produced a succession of poorish shots when he'd needed a few moderate ones to be home and dry. He reached his ball, glanced at the line of his chip, lined up and played quickly, almost as if he was trying to get the tournament over with. He knew he'd thrown it away. The ball ran on line; the pace was good. Trevino suddenly began to get very much more interested. It just might go in. And so it did. A par-5. Some said the par of the decade!

Tony was shaken. Who wouldn't be? One moment you have a fairly simple two putts for a one-stroke lead – perhaps even two – but in those few seconds the script was suddenly different and the outcome wide open once more.

Tony decided that he just wasn't going to be beaten by one final bit of luck. He'd withstood all that came at him the day before. He could still do it; a birdie and he'd still be one ahead and at worst in an eighteen-hole play-off the next day.

If this was to be, he mustn't be short. He rapped the ball firmly at the hole. It narrowly missed and ran about two-and-a-half feet past. He settled rather edgily over the ball, perhaps thinking more of what had happened seconds before rather than the job of getting the ball to the bottom of the cup. His putt missed comfortably and suddenly Trevino was again the championship leader and Jacklin finished. Soon he was able to put a brave face on it. But inside he was numb and, many would say, never the same man again.

For the record, Trevino easily parred the last hole to beat Jack Nicklaus by one stroke. Tony wasn't even second. He dropped another stroke for a 6, 5 finish and a total of 280, which put him one behind Nicklaus.

Arnold Palmer came up to Tony afterwards, with his

own memories of championships that had slipped through his fingers. 'Don't let it affect the way you think,' he said. In the commentary box we thought it was a cruel blow for Jacklin but that he'd bounce back. Great players like Palmer, Nicklaus, Jones, Hogan and others have all lost great championships and come back to fight again. Jacklin, however, couldn't make it happen. Not once in the years ahead was he amongst the contenders for a major championship. When the time came round for the Open Championship each year there was always speculation about his chances, but as the years passed such hopes needed a great deal of British optimism. Jacklin himself was to say later: 'It was certainly the biggest shock I ever had. I began to experience feelings of self-doubt. Nothing really good ever seemed to happen after Muirfield.'

As I've said, Jacklin never again featured in a major championship, but his decline in tournament play was by no means total. A few weeks after Muirfield he won the PGA Championship, and then went off to Australia and won the Dunlop International.

The following year he won the most money on the European Circuit, and was second to Peter Oosterhuis in 1974. He was still capable of brilliant play. In 1973 he won the Bogota Open against a good field by thirteen strokes, and also the Italian Open and Dunlop Masters by seven strokes, and was as dominant in the 1974 Scandinavian Enterprises Open, having an eleven-stroke margin.

Perhaps Tony always was a player of splendour and doldrums, and his peak lasted only four or five years. After 1974 his achievements were of a lesser order, the last flame coming in 1982, when he won the PGA Championship at the Hillside Golf Club, Southport, defeating Bernhard Langer in a play-off. However, in the forty years since the end of the Second World War, his is still the key name in British golf. Who can say what he would have achieved if that Muirfield championship had come his way?

6

The Two Ages of Man

Raymond Loran Floyd smiles readily as he reaches out
to take some nice prize-money or when raising a trophy
on high. Otherwise not too much. He rather has the air
of a man contemplating a bottle of whisky that has seen
better days, half empty, not half full.

How strange that this severe and sometimes gloomy
man should have once been so very different. 'Pretty
Boy' used to be his nickname on the US Tour and his
reputation was for fairly wild living, his most constant
fellow revellers through the night hours Doug Sanders
and Al Besselink. However, when playing a tournament
Raymond did try to get to bed by, let's say, 2 a.m.

When he had achieved modest success Floyd looked
for enterprises outside golf, and he settled on the
management of a group called The Ladybirds, who
claimed to be the first topless band. Well they may have
been but I can assure you there wasn't an accordionist in
sight!

Did such activities have an effect on his golfing career?
It's impossible to say. We are told that the stars practise
intensively every day, are rigidly abstemious, never cast
a glance at any woman other than their lawful spouse
and, in some cases, retire to bed at 9 p.m. with an
improving book. True enough maybe in the case of the
Caspers, Nicklauses, Millers, Players and lesser lights of
the world of golf – but there are just as many exceptions.

Floyd is very nearly an exact contemporary of Jack
Nicklaus, just a couple of years or so younger, and won

his first tournament in 1963, the season after Jack's first success. At the time he was the third youngest player to win an American tournament, just twenty years and five months old. It happened in remarkable fashion. Floyd missed the thirty-six-hole cut in all except one of his first ten entries and in the eleventh went out and won the St Petersburg Open. In his first six seasons he only won once more, but still made a living at the game. In those years he was never better than twenty-fourth on the US money list, and he had to wait until 1969 before making a great leap forward. In that year he rose to eighth position and won three tournaments. One of these was a major championship, the PGA. Although it has less prestige than the other three, Floyd really had arrived – or so it seemed. He also made his first Ryder Cup appearance at Royal Birkdale that year. In the PGA Floyd played brilliantly, his first three rounds being 69, 66 and 67 and went into the final round with a five-stroke lead. Even so, he finished only a stroke ahead of Gary Player, who had to cope with anti-Apartheid demonstrators as well as the golf course.

But if Floyd seemed to have arrived, he just as promptly disappeared. No more victories came his way until 1975, and in the early 1970s he was apt to languish around the seventieth position in the US money list.

Then came one of those happenings which supply golf writers with a paragraph or two. Sometimes, it's a new putter, rescued from neglect in a dusty corner of a pro's shop, or just as often a driver which feels just right the instant you swish the clubhead gently to and fro and like the look of the head as you set it against the ball. In Floyd's case, it was a wife. Before, he was winning just enough money to make both ends meet. Beyond that, said Floyd, 'I didn't care.'

By the beginning of 1976 he had two sons. With a family to support, he cared a great deal more about his golfing career. So, I suppose, have many others, but their careers came to nothing. The difference was that Floyd had talent and nerve, but lacked the desire to be a great player. At least he had a substitute now, the need to build a secure future. He got past $100,000 in tournament winnings in both 1974 and 1975 for the first time since his one really good year, 1969, and came to the 1976 Masters with some steady performances behind him earlier in the season.

Jack Nicklaus, who had taken his fifth Masters the previous year, made his best start ever in the event with rounds of 67 and 69, easily justifying his position as favourite. The problem for Jack, however, was that Floyd had made the best start ever in the event, scoring rounds of 65 and 66, unprecedented stuff.

He was the leader after the first round, his 65 just one shot above the course record, and already there was talk about his new 'little wood'. Floyd, like so many tournament professionals today, regards his 1-iron as a very good friend, mainly to keep tee shots on the fairway. With so little rough at Augusta, this is less vital than on many courses. Although there are trees a-plenty, they are not particularly close-packed and a line to the green can often be found after a hook or slice. Floyd had hardly used his 1-iron in recent years in the Masters both for this reason and because the club gave him too low a flight for the shots over water to the par-5s. With this relatively flat trajectory, his ball tended to skip through the greens, fatal at the 15th where there is water beyond the green as well as in front.

Just for Augusta he bought himself an 'old gentleman's persuader' – a 5-wood. It gave him about the same length as a 1-iron with a much higher flight. The theory was fine, the results even better. Floyd, in his first round, hit 5-wood shots into the 2nd, 13th and 15th greens and two-putted for his birdies at each of these par-5s. He had another birdie 4 at the 8th, the remaining par-5, without resorting to the club. He had one bogey during his round and other birdies here and there (four in a row from the 13th to the 16th).

Though Floyd was the leader, Jack Nicklaus' 67 was thought far more important. Floyd, with only one tournament win since 1969, was given just a little more chance of winning than Andy North, who lay second with a score of 66. This was hardly a compliment. North was rated as having no chance whatsoever – the odds you could have found against his becoming twice US Open Champion in the years ahead would have been astronomical.

At the end of the second day Floyd's chances were no longer being dismissed. You could hardly argue with a 65 followed by a 66 to set a new Masters thirty-six-hole record which could just possibly last as long as Henry Cotton's 67, 65 start in the 1934 British Open Championship (fifty-one years so far). This time Floyd basically made his score with a run of four under par over three holes. Using that 5-wood again he birdied the par-5 13th, had a birdie 3 on the next, and then hit a 3-wood to three feet on the 15th for an eagle. With a shot dropped on the 17th, Floyd stood at 13 under at the end of his round.

Even so, Jack Nicklaus had caught him at one point, mainly by being six under the card in his play on just three holes. He eagled the 2nd, a par-5, holed out a sand iron for a 2 on the 7th, a par-4, and finally single-putted the par-5 13th for his third eagle of the round. With his 69, he trailed Floyd by six strokes but, given his tremendous record in the Masters, still looked a likely winner.

Today Floyd has a formidable reputation as a front runner; his fellow professionals particularly respect the ability to keep going when you know you really 'ought' to win. However, Raymond was playing so well that he was actively enjoying it all. Augusta seemingly was a very friendly place and, for Floyd, all the holes looked to be fairly easy birdie opportunities. By the end of the third round he had built the biggest lead ever achieved by a Masters champion – eight strokes. Still there were those who pointed out that Ken Venturi, back in 1956, turned in an 80 in his final round to let Jack Burke win. He, too, had led Burke by eight with eighteen holes to go.

Floyd's third round 70 was two under par and not as

consistently brilliant as his first thirty-six holes had been, although only one player, Hale Irwin, bettered it with a 67 and he was already miles behind. It was far more significant that Nicklaus had a 73 to go eight behind, and another fancied player in good form that year, Ben Crenshaw, a 72 which put him eleven behind Floyd's total of 201. Floyd had birdies on two of the first four holes, but then dropped shots on the 5th and 6th. He reached the turn in 35, however, respectable enough for a man trying to maintain a lead. The 11th saw his worst moment in the whole championship. The main hazard on this par-4 is water to the left of the green, and Floyd pulled his approach shot right into it. It meant a two-over-par 6, and Raymond was one over par for the round. Larry Ziegler, who had begun with rounds of 67 and 71, momentarily pulled to within four strokes of Floyd. However, Floyd kept his composure, the 5-wood brought him another birdie on the 13th and he had two more, on the 15th and 18th for an inward nine in 35.

Floyd was now seen as the certain winner, but he was no Max Faulkner, who once signed autographs 'Max Faulkner, Open Champion, 1951' with thirty-six holes left to play. Raymond simply said, 'You know, I've still got to go out there, play the round and not get hurt.' In other words, 'Don't three-putt too often or hit into the water hazards.'

Floyd didn't do any of these things and, all things considered, had a pleasant walk round that last day. One odd and desirable record was lost early on, but that was mainly a statistic. Floyd failed to birdie the 2nd. In the first three rounds he had birdied (or eagled) each of the par-5s – 2nd, 8th, 13th and 15th – every time he played them. However, at the end of the day, he was fourteen under par on these long holes. That choice of a 5-wood was the most decisive factor in his victory. His performance on the par-5s beat the previous record, thirteen under by Jimmy Demaret, and can be compared with Jack Nicklaus' two under when winning his first Masters in 1963. For the tournament, Floyd was seventeen under par after his 72 in the last round, and his total of 271 is a record he shares with Jack Nicklaus (1965). He won by eight strokes from Ben Crenshaw with Nicklaus and Ziegler eleven behind in third place.

This overwhelming victory sent Raymond Floyd into the second stage of his career, and was in itself one of the most remarkable feats of dominance over a high-class field that I've ever seen. I was again privileged to be there several years later when he once more seized an early lead in a major championship and kept a tight grip throughout. This time it was the 1982 PGA Championship, held at Southern Hills, Tulsa, Oklahoma.

He opened with 63, which equalled the championship record. After rounds of 69 and 68, he led by five strokes going into the final round. Though this was a low-scoring event with many scores under 70, Lanny Wadkins closing with a round of 67 for second place and Fred Couples with a 66 to tie for third, Floyd was never seriously threatened and came to the last hole needing a par-4 for a total of 270 to beat the championship record. This time he did falter. He missed the green with his second shot and was left with a little pitch over a bunker. He fluffed this and so, like Gary Player in the 1959 Open Championship, ended with a 6 on the last – but was still a very comfortable winner by three strokes.

Since that Masters win, Floyd has been right amongst the leading players on the US Tour. In the 1980s alone he has won well over $1,600,000 in America. The dollars will soon be forgotten, but it is interesting that with three major championship victories to his credit he has equalled the achievements of, amongst others, Henry Cotton, Billy Casper and Tommy Armour.

7

The Great Shoot-Out

Victory after an eighteen-hole play-off with Jack Newton
in the 1975 Open Championship at Carnoustie gave
Tom Watson the beginnings of an international reputation. In America his victory counted for rather less.
There, he was more recognized as a coming man because
of his play on the US Tour where he was in the top ten
money winners both in 1974 and 1975.

He didn't *really* arrive until 1977. In that season he
doubled his total of US Tour wins by winning the Bing
Crosby, and the San Diego Open and, in April when the
Masters came around, was the choice of many to win.
But Jack Nicklaus carried the most support for he was
still without a serious rival as the number one golfer in
the world. However, Watson's performance in the Masters that year chipped away at the pedestal and at the
end it was he who came off best.

At the beginning of the final round, Watson and Ben
Crenshaw were in the lead, followed a stroke away by
Rik Massengale and then Jack Nicklaus and Jim Col-
bert, with three to make up. Crenshaw quickly faded, but
both Massengale and Watson reached the turn in 32 to
Nicklaus' 33. The final pairings were Watson and
Massengale, Crenshaw and Nicklaus. The players out
last at Augusta can easily see what the others are doing.
Watson had to watch Jack sink quite a long putt to save
his par on the 11th but followed that with a birdie on the
12th. As Watson had dropped a shot on the 10th, his lead
was cut to just one stroke. When Nicklaus birdied the

13th as well, Watson, from the centre of the fairway knew they were level but moments later went ahead with a birdie of his own.

The betting had been that Watson, with a reputation for 'choking' in major championships, would be the most likely of the leaders to crack. He hadn't and Nicklaus was only getting on terms by producing a typical last-round charge. He maintained his momentum with a par (Watson followed with a bogey) on the 14th and a birdie at the 15th, which gave him the lead for a short time until Watson equalled those scores.

The pair were level with just three holes left to play. This was roughly the same position from which Nicklaus had gone on to defeat Johnny Miller and Tom Weiskopf in the 1975 Masters. Much of the credit for that win must go to the forty-five-foot putt he holed at the par-3 16th, but this time he took two putts, as did Watson, whose iron shot had given him a reasonable opportunity for a birdie.

Nicklaus *nearly* birdied the 17th and the difference, and virtual winning of the championship, was that Watson did. Ahead, playing the 18th, Nicklaus had to birdie the hole for a record-equalling round of 64. Instead, he bunkered his second, took 5 for a 66 and Watson, with a final 67, was the winner.

This was probably a far more significant victory in Watson's career than his Carnoustie championship. There he had posted his score, and all the contenders except Jack Newton fell away. At Augusta Nicklaus had come at him head on with a great final round. He overtook Watson and even went into the lead, despite the fact that Watson was playing an excellent round himself. For the final four holes Tom was two under par with birdie putts on all the holes. There was no doubt he had *won* the Masters. Many championships are 'given' to you, or perhaps, as Nicklaus has put it, happen when a player fails a little less than the rest.

The final nine holes at Augusta are as severe a test of a champion's nerve as you can find anywhere. The 10th is

71

a long par-4 curving downhill followed by another difficult 4 of which Hogan said: 'Any time I'm on the green in two, I've hit a bad shot.' With water encroaching on the left the great man liked to play to the right of the green. The 12th, 13th, 15th and 16th all have water blocking the route to the green. No recovery is possible from either a poor shot or bad judgement, and the nerve needed to hit over the water at the 13th and 15th is considerable when the player knows he can play short with his second shot and then try to pitch and single-putt for his birdie.

Yes, there had definitely been a shoot-out at Augusta, but an even more enthralling one lay three months ahead in Scotland on the Ayrshire coast.

The venue was Turnberry, never before used for the Open Championship and the first course to be added to the rota since Royal Birkdale in 1940 and Royal Portrush in Northern Ireland in 1951. Birkdale was not used, because of the Second World War, until 1954 and the Portrush event was a one-off. I'm sure Turnberry is here to stay, and indeed the championship was played there again in 1986.

Golf first came to Turnberry in 1903 when thirteen holes were laid out, and the large hotel which overlooks the sea and the course was completed just a few years later. Many changes were made to the course over the years, the most drastic coming during the Second World War when the dunes were flattened and concrete runways laid: an RAF Coastal Command training base was needed much more than a golf course!

After the war the Ailsa championship course was constructed, and also another fine course, the Arran. Together, they make a very fine thirty-six holes, though only the dramatic Ailsa is used for the Open Championship, plus a tee from the Arran to make the last hole a more testing dogleg. The firm of Alliss and Thomas was called in by the R and A to advise on changes to improve its championship qualities. Though only a small part of our scheme was actually carried out, the scoring in easy

72

conditions in 1977 showed what a good test Turnberry is. Writing before the 1986 championship, I am eager to see what the stars make of it, if a good wind gets up, as at Royal St George's in 1985.

Conditions were easy for the 1977 championship for two reasons. The rough was not severe, almost a joke, to Americans used to seeing their ball settle well down, even in the semi-rough, in most US Open and PGA championships. The trouble was a drought, which followed on the fine summer of 1976, reducing the rough to tufty wispy patches from which players could usually fire a long iron or whatever at the green, rather than have to wedge back to the fairway.

A links also needs some wind: for they are so often hard and fast running by July. Even a long par-4 can become just a drive and a flick. There was very little breeze except on the final morning at Turnberry in 1977, and what there was came from the wrong direction, the northeast rather than the prevailing southwest. Too many holes became just a drive and a pitch, and even one of the par-5s, the 17th, played as no more than a drive and mid-iron. But, as we shall see in this memorable shoot-out, only two players came close to making a mockery of Turnberry; the rest of the field most certainly didn't and the majority were beaten by it. Par on the card was 70, but as both of the par-5s, the 7th and the 17th, were reachable in two, I would put it at 68 for all four days.

On the first day the championship committee decided on difficult pin placings not, for example, particularly tight to hazards but on awkward slopes. Two strokes of equal quality could result in an 'easy' birdie putt up a little slope or have a player thinking more about how he was going to stop his six-footer near the hole. Towards the end of the day, it looked as if a young English hopeful would lead the field with a 67 but then, at 9.20 p.m., John Schroeder came in with a brilliant 66. His play aroused tremendous interest for he was the son of a famous father, Ted Schroeder, a double open champion whose stamping grounds had been Forest Hills and Wimbledon, not Baltusrol and St Andrews.

But where, meanwhile, were the big guns? Doing very nicely thank you. Trevino, Nicklaus and Watson were all round in 68. Nicklaus' score had given the most trouble. He dropped a stroke at the 2nd, and then ran up a 6. His 37 to the turn was not good. But Nicklaus has always been great at putting a bad shot or a poor spell of play quickly behind him. On the 10th he faced one of the most difficult holes of the day, over 450 yards, tightly bunkered and playing into the breeze. Nicklaus scored a perfect 3, and then birdied the 11th as well. He was back in 31 with a long putt for another birdie at the last.

Watson made his 68 more easily. His driving was particularly good, long and well placed, leaving him the best lines into the flags. There seemed no reason why he shouldn't have had a 64 or 65 except that his putter was not working as well as usual. He also dropped a shot on the 18th where he missed the green, chipped not too well and missed a five-foot putt.

For the second day the course was at the mercy of the players. There was little or no wind, sun blazed down and the pin placements had been eased. Thirteen players were under par, compared with seven on the first day. The most below par was Mark Hayes, a man experimenting with the reversed-hands putting grip. It hadn't worked too well in Hayes' first round when he had a 76, but his 63 was exceptional and broke the championship record first set by Henry Cotton at Royal St George's forty-three years earlier. On the 18th tee Hayes had only 4s, 3s and one 2 on his card, but then bunkered his tee shot and eventually took 5. At one point it had looked as if the US Open Champion Hubert Green might do even better. At the 4th, a par-3 of 170 yards with a steep bank down to the beach on the left and the green cut into the side of a sand dune, he hit a rather poor 6-iron that caught the bank on the right. Instead of staying there and leaving him an awkward chip, it skipped down and dropped into the hole, a 1 that helped Green to reach the turn in 32. He then birdied the next four holes, but dropped shots on both the 14th and 16th. However, he had the 17th to come. How many golf courses have a weak finishing hole because the designer had to get the players back to the clubhouse some way or another, while there are a host of good 17ths (think, if you like of the 17th and 18th at St Andrews). The 17th at Turnberry is a fair hole, with an inviting drive from an elevated tee to a valley fairway. For the club golfer, if he gets a good tee shot away, there is the prospect of getting up to this par-5 of 500 yards in two. The championship competitors, however, were making rather a nonsense of it. It was playing no more than a drive and a medium iron. There were eagles a plenty, and everyone in the field knew he had failed if he didn't birdie the hole. Hubert didn't. He hooked his tee shot, knocked his second into the solitary fairway bunker and ended up with a 6. He was round in 66, but what might have been when you think he was seven under par with five to play.

These rounds from Hayes and Green, with a 65 from Angel Gallardo of Spain and Roger Maltbie's 66, which gave him the championship lead incidentally, were a hint to Watson and Nicklaus of what could happen. They hadn't benefited from the conditions, both taking 70 to be one stroke behind. Nicklaus began with birdies on two of the first three holes, but took three putts on both the 6th and 10th and missed from about four feet on the 14th. Later in the day Watson had the same score, without much in the way of either alarms or fireworks.

So far, then, the two had identical scores. Long was it to continue but it wasn't yet a Nicklaus *versus*Watson battle. Many players were still in it:

Maltbie   137
Watson, Nicklaus, Trevino and Green   138
Hayes, Peter Butler   139
Ben Crenshaw, George Burns, Seve Ballesteros, Schroeder, Howard Clark and C. S. Hsu   140

So four strokes covered thirteen players, and many

more were on 141, 142 and 143. By the end of the third day it was all to look very different, a two-horse race with one outsider perhaps worth a bet, Ben Crenshaw.

The weather was again exceptionally fine, with scarcely a breath of wind, when the leaders went out. Nicklaus and Watson, both on 138, were drawn together by a happy chance which did much to add to the drama of the final thirty-six holes. A cracking start they both made, Nicklaus beginning with birdies on the 1st, 4th, 6th and 7th. Watson, for his part, birdied the 3rd, 4th and 7th, but there was a two-stroke swing on the par-3 6th, where Watson took 4 to Nicklaus' 2. Nicklaus was 31 to the turn, Watson 34. They both came away with birdies on the difficult 10th, and went through the next three holes in par figures before Nicklaus faltered at the 14th, taking three putts (perhaps his Achilles heel in this championship?). Watson drew level when he had a 2 at the 15th, and the 17th yielded birdies to both, Nicklaus coming away a little cross. He had missed from six feet for an eagle 3. The cut and thrust was kept up to the very last. Here Watson looked to have an advantage putting for a birdie, while Nicklaus had sent his second shot just through the green. Watson came close to holing his birdie putt, but Jack's par was good enough after he had played a most delicate chip to about six inches, which looked at one time as if it might drop.

Both were round in 65, a score equalled by Tommy Horton. He had started out seven strokes behind the leader, Roger Maltbie, who played well enough for a 72, a score he might have expected to be good enough to keep his lead, but in fact left him six strokes behind the leaders at the end of the day. This was the position with eighteen to go:

Nicklaus and Watson   203
Crenshaw   206
Maltbie, Horton and Gaylord Burrows   209
Trevino and Johnny Miller   210

Of those who had started out the day near the top of

the field, only Ben Crenshaw had matched the panache of Nicklaus and Watson with a round of 66. The winner surely had to come from one these three. No one else could play round Turnberry seven strokes or more better than *both* Nicklaus and Watson. So far, this pair had identical rounds of 68, 70, 65. Neither could afford to play defensively in each other's company, so even a score of 65 in the last round from one of those trailing was very unlikely to be good enough. Nicklaus had been playing superbly, but I thought Watson was striking the ball even better. His driving was more impressive, both for length and accuracy, and his putting looked foolproof. But perhaps Jack had the edge with the irons.

In the Press tent, Watson spoke like a man who knew he'd arrived. There was almost a touch of arrogance. He thought his 65 was the better round of the two. He had struck the ball better and had missed fewer fairways. And perhaps Jack had been fortunate with the lies he had found in the rough. Nicklaus said rather less. For years he'd seen all the challengers come and go – Weiskopf, Miller, Jacklin and we could add Player and Trevino. Watson was merely the most recent of a long line of pretenders to his throne.

The final day was again fine, but with a breeze early on which sent many scores into the high 70s. Crenshaw almost made the perfect start when he put his second shot on the 1st only a couple of yards from the hole. However, he missed the putt but played on steadily until he took 6 at the 9th. That really put him out of the championship, especially when he went on to drop shots at the 10th, 12th and 14th. The winner by then had to be Watson or Nicklaus – but which?

Nicklaus, as in the third round, soon took an early lead. At both the 1st and 2nd holes Nicklaus was in the rough and Watson up the middle and longer, but it was Jack who came out best. Nicklaus, with a chance of a birdie on the 1st from about four yards, missed. Watson, only some two yards away, pushed his birdie attempt wide of the hole. On the 2nd, Jack had a heavy lie for his second shot and debated long over the choice of club before getting his ball some three yards from the hole. Watson, from a much better position, pulled his shot a touch and ran off the green to the left. Watson, the master at getting up and down in two, then tried a little lob which finished well short of the hole. And when he missed the putt he was one over par for the round. Nicklaus holed his birdie putt to go into a very useful two-stroke lead.

He increased this on the short 4th with yet another birdie. At nine under par to Watson's six under, he was showing signs of pulling away while, ahead, Ben Crenshaw had yet to fade completely from contention. At this point he was just a stroke worse than Watson.

The contest for second place didn't last long. Watson made a crucial move, with birdies at the 5th, 7th and 8th to catch Nicklaus, although he then immediately dropped a shot at the 9th to reach the turn in 34 to Jack's 33. At both the 10th and 11th Nicklaus held temporary advantages. On the 10th Watson was short in two and then chipped two yards past, but managed to match Nicklaus' par-4. At the short 11th Jack put his tee shot in close, while Watson was bunkered short of the green but recovered brilliantly to get his par.

On they went, Nicklaus still with that one-stroke lead, which he increased with a birdie on the 12th after he had driven into a fairly heavy lie in the rough. Again with a two-stroke lead, he drove into the rough on the 13th and Watson, from the fairway, was this time rewarded for a good iron shot with a putt from about three yards which he holed. Only one in it now. At the next both had opportunities for birdies, Watson from considerably closer, but both missed.

The 15th, some 220 yards, was one of two holes that governed the destiny of the championship. Watson, with the honour, hit his tee shot poorly. He was short and left, several yards off the green in semi-rough. Nicklaus' tee shot was also not so good, just clearing a bunker which lay between him and the flag. He was left with a reasonable chance of a birdie, while Watson faced a difficult chip to save his par-3. However, from twenty-five yards or so he decided to putt through the rough fringe and across the green. It was to be as decisive a shot as that little lob on the 71st hole at Pebble Beach which won him the 1982 US Open Championship. Watson holed both in very unlikely fashion. When Nicklaus failed with his putt, the two were square for the first time since the 2nd green. Nicklaus had twice led and had twice been caught.

The 16th is a par-4 of just over 400 yards with a burn wandering across immediately short and right of the green. Watson had the advantage after the tee shots. His was a superb drive while Nicklaus' was pushed slightly to the right, leaving him the more difficult line in to the flag. However, his approach was perfect for distance, if a little wide. Watson pitched well past the flag and they settled for par-4s.

On the 17th Watson again drove well, but Nicklaus was not to be outdone this time. He made perfect contact and hit an enormous shot. At this 500-yard par-5, he needed just a 7-iron for his second shot. However, it had to be played under some pressure for Watson, playing first, hit a splendid shot right at the flag, stopping perhaps five yards past. Nicklaus' 7-iron was not hit with great conviction. Perhaps he felt he had too much club. The result was he struck the ball a bit heavy and pushed it as well. He finished some twenty yards short of the green and a little to the right. Watson was a certainty for a birdie at the worst. Jack had to get down in two if he was to avoid going one behind with only the last hole to play. For a while it looked as if he'd do it, running his ball to within four or five feet. When he putted for his 4, Watson had already missed his eagle putt. Jack took his time. His putting stroke was firm. The ball didn't even touch the hole. Watson was a stroke in the lead and smashed his tee shot with a long iron straight down the middle at the 431-yard 18th. He was, he later declared, precisely 178 yards from the flag.

Jack Nicklaus wanted to be a great deal nearer than that, so took out his driver hoping to have just a pitch left for his second. Alas, he hit a poor drive, wide and to the right, heading for gorse bushes. However, the shot didn't cost him the championship there and then for his ball came to rest a couple of feet or so short of trouble. He was still in business. But not for long. Watson hit as pure a 7-iron as I've ever seen, right at the flag, biting and stopping only a couple of feet, perhaps only eighteen inches away. He'd surely won.

But Nicklaus wasn't ready to concede. He took great care with his difficult second and succeeded in getting his ball on to the green, something like fifteen yards from the hole. However, Watson was sitting almost stone dead – though even that length of putt can be missable if you have to get it to win. Unbelievably Nicklaus holed his long putt, and for a few moments there was a chance that this unparalleled contest would go to an eighteen-hole play-off the next day. Watson put such thoughts from his mind and went briskly to his ball and tapped it firmly into the hole. A 65 for Watson, a 66 for Jack.

A hatful of scoring records had gone, with Jack Nicklaus now in second place for all of them. Watson had beaten the record aggregate for the Open Championship by no fewer than two strokes *per round* (268 to 276). His two 65s to finish were the lowest thirty-six holes recorded in any of the four major championships (beating Johnny Miller's 65, 66 in the 1975 US Masters). His last round 65 was the lowest final round by a champion (again eclipsing Miller, who came off the last green at Royal Birkdale in 1976 with a 66).

I could go on but this great contest shouldn't be seen as a matter of statistics, even though some should last for a very long time. Simply, it was a great match and it made Tom Watson both the world's number one and eligible to be considered one of the few all-time greats.

8

Back to the Top

On 13 April 1975 Gary Player, the previous year's Masters Champion, helped Jack Nicklaus into the traditional green jacket at Augusta. It was Jack's fifth victory in the event and his sixteenth major championship. A little over three years later, Jack held aloft for the third time the old claret jug which has been the Open Championship trophy since 1872. He had completed a slam of all four major championships for the third time.

The fifth Masters victory seemed to show that all was well in Jack's world. In beating Johnny Miller and Tom Weiskopf into second place by a single stroke he had, at least temporarily, dismissed the two closest rivals to his pre-eminence in world golf. The future was to reveal that Weiskopf would not add to his solitary major championship triumph, the 1973 British Open, and that Miller, though winning his second major championship at Royal Birkdale in 1976, would fall right away from the superb standards he had set in the 1974 and 1975 seasons. In 1978 he won just $17,000 on the US Tour and was 111th on the money list. Despite some recovery in the 1980s he was by then just a good, not great, player.

Meanwhile, Nicklaus was having troubles of his own. As he began the 1980 season, he had won only one major championship in five years and had just experienced his worst year since turning professional back in 1961. Never previously out of the top four in US money winnings, Jack finished seventy-first in 1979 with a mere $59,000 after averaging well over $250,000 for the previous eight years. The headlines he made were all of failures, though he did manage a fourth place in the Masters and tied for second with Ben Crenshaw, three behind Seve Ballesteros, in the British Open.

Was it all inevitable, a result of the passing of the years? After all, Jack celebrated his fortieth birthday on 21 January 1980. Nicklaus himself didn't think so. Forty years before, Byron Nelson examined his stroke-by-stroke performance for a season of high excellence, decided he could do a very great deal better if he eliminated the 'silly' shots and did just that.

Nicklaus had always known that his technical strengths were long and usually reliable driving, excellence at hitting greens with full shots and good sound putting, especially on fast championship greens and under pressure. In his practice sessions, Jack devoted most of his time to improving his strengths and little to his weak points. He had never been a better than average bunker player, but a greater weakness was in the half shots and touch play needed when a player misses a green. He felt a moderate pitch and run, lob, chip or bump and run would do. His putting wouldn't let him down.

Do you remember how Nicklaus played the last hole at St Andrews in the 1978 Open Championship? He drove well and was left with a full pitch with a wedge or 9-iron to the flag. Alternatively, he could run the ball up and on to the green. Well, the Scots do like to see a man play the pitch and run and perhaps that's why Nicklaus did so, a runner with a 7-iron. A roar went up from the huge gallery. Undoubtedly the shot was a great public relations success, made easy by the fact he was two shots ahead of the field.

Yet it wasn't a good one. It was struck much too firmly and finished at the back of the green, about eighteen yards past the hole – not a position Jack would have relished if he'd needed to get down in two to win over the four players who tied for second place: Ray Floyd, Tom Kite, Simon Owen and Ben Crenshaw. It was a little clumsy but it didn't matter, and Nicklaus did get down in two putts.

After the 1979 season, Nicklaus decided to go 'back to school'. He took lessons on the full swing from his teacher since the age of ten – Jack Grout – and in February 1980 had Phil Rodgers to stay with him for two weeks at his home in Florida. Grout helped Nicklaus to get the power back into his full shots, while Rodgers worked with Nicklaus on his short game. Jack learned to use something very like his putting stroke for the little chip shots from the fringe and to play them with 'fairly dead hands and wrists'. For short pitch shots he decided to use more rather than less hand action.

Nicklaus emerged feeling he had more understanding of the short game and a greater range of shots than ever before. But there was no magic solution. We didn't see Nicklaus storming through the field on the US Tour. Historically the Masters is his best event, apart from his consistently high placings in the British Open. Nicklaus was under par in only one of his rounds and finished thirty-third, a distant sixteen strokes behind Seve Ballesteros. Before the US Open at Baltusrol came round, Nicklaus had played in nine events and had finished in the top ten only once when he had a strong finish in mid-March in the Doral-Eastern Open in Florida. His final round 69 was equalled by only two other players on a windy day but Ray Floyd beat it, his 66 enabling him to come from behind to tie Nicklaus and then win the sudden death play-off.

Nicklaus's form in this event seemed a one-off performance. As the Open neared, he came twentieth in his own Memorial tournament at the end of May and then, in the Atlanta Classic, started with a round of 78 and missed the thirty-six-hole cut. However, his second-round 67 was encouraging.

Nicklaus was about to turn his year into one of his great ones and to set several new records. The first came on 12 June 1980 when he played the lowest first round ever in a major championship, a 63 which equalled the

My father in 1936 – a simple, sweet swing

Not bad, not bad at all! Myself in 1962

Ah, it looks simple – but! One of the many, many putters I tried

The start of a new British golfing era – Tony Jacklin goes for a big one from the rough in the 1969 Open at Lytham

Peter Thomson, the best over-50s player in the world in 1985 and still a superb hitter of the ball

Gary Player – the most tenacious of them all. He is still good enough to compete at any age level and is sure to be a huge success amongst the over-50s

One of Arnold's better finishes, played at his peak in the early '60s

Oh, thank you Lord! Trevino drops a long putt

Yet another joyous Nicklaus day, this time the 1980 US Open

But there were others

When Watson became the world's number one. The Open Championship at Turnberry in 1977

The game is in safe hands as long as there are some Crenshaws about

At last – a major victory for Ben Crenshaw. Sinking the final putt to win the 1984 US Masters

Any very good player can win one major; the second takes some doing. Fuzzy Zoeller has done just that

Get past that one if you can! Greg Norman has been a star for several years but his first major championship has still eluded him

The touch of a master. Seve at St Andrews for the 1984 Open

What am I doing over here? Tom knows it's all over as he plays his third shot at the Road hole in the 1984 Open at St Andrews

Ballesteros tells the Press how he feels after his second Open Championship victory in 1984

That nervous chip by Lyle at
the last hole at Royal St
George's in 1985

Don't say it's going to come
back to my feet!

Oh Gawd, it has . . .

Now what on earth do I do?

Were you worried? So was I, but all's well in the end

US Open record for any round set by Johnny Miller when he came from behind to win the 1973 US Open. Oddly he didn't start off at all well. His par on the 1st was followed by a bogey on the second hole. He got that stroke back immediately at the 3rd, and with two more birdies reached the turn in 32, two under par. The real fireworks came on the second nine, which he played in five under par, just thirty-one strokes. After a par at the 10th, he had three birdies in a row and five in all, missing from little more than a yard on the last when a round of 62 was there for the taking.

Tom Weiskopf had finished earlier with a 63 of his own, after also dropping a shot on the first hole. Nicklaus hadn't needed many of his new short-game techniques. He had been on the green in regulation figures at fifteen of the holes and needed only twenty-seven putts, single-putting ten of the greens.

Neither player could be expected to go on like this. On the second day, Weiskopf struck the ball equally well, but seemed to drop a shot every time he missed a green. He was round in 75, which eventually put him four strokes behind the lead, Nicklaus' 71 and gave him a total of 134, a two-round record for the championship.

Nicklaus began his second round at breakfast time looking as if he might put the result beyond doubt before lunch when he birdied both the 1st and 3rd, each stiff par-4s well over 400 yards. Flaws crept in later though. He took three putts on the 6th, and dropped shots after being in bunkers on both the 11th and 12th. The 12th was a disaster hole. Bunkered in the face short of this 190-yard par-3, Nicklaus got out into rough and then hit a little wedge shot too hard. Luck was with him, however, when his ball caught the hole which stopped its race through the back of the green. He then two-putted for a 5. His position against par for the championship had gone from nine under after the 3rd to five under. One of those make-or-break putts that are so much a Nicklaus speciality followed minutes later. On the 13th, his first putt was from six or seven yards. He raced it past

the hole, leaving himself a putt of about six feet coming back. If he missed, four shots would have been gone in three holes – but he didn't. The rot was stopped and Nicklaus parred all the remaining holes, except the monster 630-yard 17th where he got a putt of similar length for a birdie and finished in 71.

There was a similar moment of truth in Jack's third round. It came on the 15th. He had just dropped a shot after bunkering his second to the 14th and then drove well right. However, he went down the shaft and played a knocked-down shot to some five yards of the flag. The par looked saved yet Jack came close to four-putting. His first was very timid and came to rest about six feet short. His second overcompensated and he went a dangerous three feet past. Infinite care and nerve saw that one into the middle of the hole.

By this time, Nicklaus was by no means running away with the championship. He had started out the first day in the company of Gene Littler and Isao Aoki. The Japanese was still with Nicklaus for the third round, having tied for second place after thirty-six holes, two behind the championship leader with 136 to Jack's 134. His putting with that wristy stroke, the toe of his centreshaft high in the air, was a good part of the reason. Aoki had used only sixty-five putts after two-and-a-half rounds of golf. He had no three-putts until the second hole of the final round, and that was his only one throughout. In his second-round 68, Aoki putted just twenty-three times and single-putted eight of the last nine greens. All this after using his putter just twenty-seven times in his first round.

After the first nine holes, Nicklaus had increased his lead over the Japanese to three. On the 13th and 14th, however, Aoki gained two strokes on Nicklaus, but the gap was back to two when Aoki bunkered his tee shot to the 16th, a par-3 of over 200 yards, where Jack struck a sumptuous long iron to about three yards but failed with his putt.

His momentum continued with a good drive at the

630-yard 17th, where Aoki pulled his tee shot into a bunker. He found a good lie, and was able to clear the cross bunkers ahead with a 5-iron. However, he was still nearly 200 yards from the green. Nicklaus, in an ideal position, then duffed a fairway wood shot and was lucky to miss the bunkers. His next shot was from far less favourable a place, the ball was well below his feet and there was still 175 yards to go. The swing and strike this time, with a 4-iron were good and he had the chance of a birdie with a putt of about ten feet. Aoki sent his third shot about ten yards from the hole, but struck the birdie putt too firmly. No matter, it hit the back of the hole, jumped inches into the air, and fell in. On the last hole, 543 yards, Aoki's putter once again had the better of it. Nicklaus was on the fringe in two, but took three more after sending his first putt a couple of yards past while Aoki deliberately played his second shot short of bunkers and rough, pitched up to about five yards and, of course, holed the putt for his birdie 4.

Nicklaus had been caught. The 63 was history, but another record had been set. Their totals of 204 were a fifty-four-hole record for the US Open. This is how the leaders stood:

Jack Nicklaus	63, 71, 70	204
Isao Aoki	68, 68, 68	204
Lon Hinkle	66, 70, 69	205
Tom Watson	71, 68, 67	206
Mark Hayes	66, 71, 69	206
Keith Fergus	66, 70, 70	206

Of the pursuers, Watson, having a superb US season, had entered the championship as favourite. Was it a sign of what might lie ahead that Watson was scoring lower each round and each of the contenders had outscored Jack Nicklaus over the last thirty-six holes?

In the fourth round, however, Nicklaus was at his best. I have never seen his composure better than that day. His 68 was bettered by only one man, Andy North, and he was far out of contention.

On the 2nd, Aoki, as I've said, took three putts for the first time and fell one stroke behind. The margin became two when Jack birdied the 3rd. At the end of nine holes, the position was the same. Jack had come through a bad patch with fairly poor drives on the 6th, 7th and 8th, but he dropped only one stroke to par on this stretch.

Championships nowadays are usually settled over the last nine holes, and on 15 June 1980 I saw Jack's long game at its best. Not only did he hold every fairway with his drives, but his placement was also excellent with Aoki's wristy tee shots always many yards behind. From ideal fairway positions, Jack then proceeded to hit every green. Even so, Aoki hung on. On the 10th, for instance, with Jack almost dead in two, he chipped in from the back fringe so that both had 3s on the 450-yarder. And so it went on. Well as Nicklaus played, Aoki was still only two strokes behind as they came to the 17th tee for the last two par-5s that might yield birdies from good pitch shots. Nicklaus hit one of his best drives of the week, played up short of trouble in front of the green and then pitched to six or seven yards. Aoki, however, put his third shot only about six feet away and later, as everyone expected, knocked it in. Before that Nicklaus had made the championship almost secure by holing his medium-length putt for a birdie.

On the 18th Jack played conservatively with a 3-wood from the tee, and then lagged a 4-iron short before a low wedge to about three yards. Aoki hit a poor second shot but wedged beautifully – it looked almost in for a moment and missed the hole by about an inch before stopping little more than three feet away. That was the end of the championship. Nicklaus didn't need his putt but got it. So, as a matter of routine, did Aoki even after a green invasion by Jack's fans. Nicklaus' 272 had beaten the previous Open record by three strokes, and Aoki also won a $50,000 prize offered to anyone who broke the record.

This is how they finished:

Nicklaus	272
Aoki	274
Watson	276
Fergus	276
Hinkle	276
Hayes	280
‑Reid	280

Nicklaus had become the fourth man to win the US Open four times, the others being Willie Anderson early this century, Bobby Jones between 1923 and 1930 and Ben Hogan in the years 1948 to 1953. The long gap of eighteen years between this win and his first in 1962 was another Nicklaus record.

Just over a month later he was at Muirfield for the Open Championship, eager for his fourth victory. He played well, apart from a first round of 73 and that was burden enough. This was an even lower-scoring championship than Baltusrol, with a 64 from Tom Watson in the third round scotching everyone.

Jack's next engagement of note was at the Oak Hill Country Club in New York State for the PGA Championship. This was the course where Lee Trevino first found the limelight by winning the 1968 US Open. Trevino had all four rounds under 70, and his total of 275 tied the championship record. The members didn't much care for this. It's the same at golf clubs the world over. The average club golfer would delight to see a top-class field struggling to break 80 and the winner averaging 75s over his home course. He appreciates its difficulties (for him!) and likes to think it's a push-over for no one.

The United States Golf Association played its part, letting it be known that Oak Hill, a Donald Ross of Dornoch design, wouldn't be considered for the Open until it had been made more difficult. Changes were made and, for the PGA, deep rough allowed to grow just short of many of the greens. If a player was straight but short, he was even more heavily penalized than for being off line and – even more debatable – the pitch-and-run shot was ruled out. The conventional rough was also severe, with just a few feet mown to about four inches in length and then what professionals call 'unplayable', meaning that if you can find your ball, all you do is hack back to the fairway. Oak Hill measured 6964 yards, playing its full length because the fairways were soft. The two par-5s, the 4th, 570 yards long, and the 13th, 596 yards, would not yield easy birdies – they were out of range for all in two shots. The greens were extremely fast.

In other words, the qualities required to win would be long, straight hitting and a good touch on the greens. It was Augusta with rough; no player of second rank was given a real chance; it was thought that no one would be under par at the finish.

Jack Nicklaus junior had a considerable influence on the outcome. He was Nicklaus' third teacher of the year and had noticed a fault that had come into the great man's putting stroke. In a recent practice round, young Jack pointed out that Nicklaus was not 'finishing his stroke', a way of saying that he was quitting on the putt before he struck the ball. Nicklaus had been putting very poorly and seized on his son's tip, which proved an instant cure.

He began with an even par round of 70, and was quietly delighted. The reason? It was a very good 70. The irons had usually been right for line and length, which left him with many birdie opportunities yet he made hardly any. Surely putting was still the problem then? The answer was 'No'. It had just been one of those days when putts struck well, with good judgement of pace and borrow, just didn't drop.

Craig Stadler was the first-day leader, a former US Amateur Champion and Walker Cup player who served a fairly long apprenticeship on the US Tour before emerging in 1980 with two tournament victories. He was round in 67, for a one-stroke lead from a bunch of players.

On the second day Nicklaus played poor golf. He was, he said, 'All over the place.' The result was that he moved into second place on 139 with Lon Hinkle, a stroke behind Gil Morgan. The difference was on the greens. He'd continued to putt well, and this time the ball fell into the hole rather than spun off the edge. In his 69 he had two bogeys, three birdies and had saved par five times with good single-putt greens. Stadler was almost gone with a round of 75, and was to finish the tournament with one of the worst rounds of the last day, an 81.

In the third round Nicklaus made his move early, holing a putt of close on twenty yards on the 1st for a birdie, and then hitting his long iron on the 3rd to about six inches. This gave him a three-stroke lead on Gil Morgan. He faltered on the 5th, where he hit a tree with his tee shot, bogied the hole and was caught by Lon Hinkle. On the 7th, however, a medium-length birdie putt made him leader for good. He completed the outward nine in 32 and was three ahead of the field, and then went on to birdie the 10th, 11th and 13th. Suddenly, he seemed in total command of the championship, seven strokes in the lead.

But the day wasn't finished. At the 15th he made his first real error when he three-putted, and followed that with a bad tee shot at the 16th. Jack usually drives with fade but the ball doesn't always behave itself. This time he hit a big hook that headed for the out of bounds. Luck was with him. The ball clattered against a fence and stayed in. He preserved his par with a good putt. Although he struggled on the last two holes, he dropped only one shot. Nicklaus was quite glad to get off the course. He had played a few poor shots but ended up with 66. He was three ahead of Hinkle, with Gil Morgan and Andy Bean six strokes behind his three-round total of 205.

On the final day Nicklaus parred the first three holes, and that was good enough to stretch his lead over Hinkle to five strokes. Almost error free and with no birdies on his card, he reached the turn in level par-35 with Hinkle and Bean still five behind. Early in the second nine, Jack increased his lead to eight over Hinkle and nine over Andy Bean. These two were now playing for second place while Nicklaus relished his triumphal progress. He dropped a shot at the 17th, but what did it matter? The tournament had been over for a couple of hours. Jack finished in 69 for a seven-stroke victory, easily the biggest margin in the history of the PGA Championship as a strokeplay event since 1958. Andy Bean was second, one over par, to Jack's six under total.

It was Nicklaus' fifth PGA Championship and his nineteenth major championship (including his two US Amateur victories). He joined Gene Sarazen and Ben Hogan as the only players to win the US Open and PGA in the same year. And think of such great names as Sam Snead, Tom Watson and Arnold Palmer. None of them have both titles in their career record.

In the five years after, Jack didn't add to his toll of major victories and won only twice in the US Tour – the 1982 Colonial National Invitation and his own Memorial Tournament at Muirfield Village, Ohio, in 1984 when he drove out of bounds near the end but won the play-off against Andy Bean.

Even in his mid-forties, Nicklaus hasn't experienced as bad a year as 1979 and is still very much to be reckoned with. He has the golf game and nerve to go on competing at the highest level as long as he cares to. Then he will put his clubs away. I don't think we'll see him on the US Seniors Tour. Jack has always wanted to be the best, not the best over fifty-year-old golfer. But who knows . . .

However, after poor performances early in his 1986 campaign, which caused one writer to declare Jack was, 'done, through, washed up and finished', he began to find his game a week before the US Masters began. Nicklaus conceded the writer had a point but resolved to show what he could do. The immediate result was only a first round of 74 but thereafter his scores came plummeting down – 71, 69 and as great a round as he has ever played, a 65 to take the championship.

He began the final day still unconsidered, four behind the leader, Greg Norman, with other players who included Seve Ballesteros, Bernhard Langer, Tom Watson, Tom Kite and Nick Price (fresh from breaking the course record with a 63) between him and the lead. After eight holes he hadn't improved his position at all. He had hit a couple of drives into trees, three putted once and stood level par for the day.

Then he began to make it happen with three birdies in a row before falling back with a shot dropped on the 12th. Thereafter, he played magnificently and suddenly became a factor in the Masters when he eagled the 15th to go to seven under and tied for 2nd place. Now he was in with a chance if he could finish strongly, and he did just that with birdies on the 16th and 17th. The rest couldn't match him and he came home by a stroke for his sixth Masters title.

In his last ten holes he had six birdies and one eagle. It should be another five years before anyone again dares to say Jack is 'done, through, washed up and finished.'

9

Crenshaw Makes His Own History

Ben Crenshaw is a member of the museum committee of the United States Golf Association and also of the Golf Collectors' Society, where he lists his interests as 'Art and Books'. When this side of the Atlantic for the Open Championship, he does another kind of collecting – golf courses. He loves to visit some of the classic courses of Scotland, England and Ireland, especially those that go back a century or more and have changed very little. I remember a few years ago we at the BBC had the idea of showing Crenshaw and Jack Nicklaus playing with hickory shafts and guttie balls. Ben delighted in the challenge; Jack didn't cope at all well.

With this interest in the history of golf, it's not surprising that Crenshaw reveres the major events because of their connections with the past. Most of all he craves an Open Championship victory, and once said, 'I really do not think I could go on living if I thought I would not win the Open Championship at St Andrews.' (Though, I suspect he'd not turn up his nose at victory on some other course!)

Equally, a US Open or Masters Championship would have been very much to Ben's taste. The first dates back to 1895 but the Masters is quite a newcomer, only fifty years old. By 1984 it had built up impressive traditions, helped by the name of Bobby Jones and the fact that the championship is always held on the same course each year, the Augusta National in the state of Georgia.

When Crenshaw came into professional golf in 1973, it

looked as if one of these titles would fall to him very soon. More was expected of him than any ex-amateur since Jack Nicklaus had begun playing for money more than ten years earlier. While at the University of Texas he had won the National Collegiate Championship three times, the Western Amateur and Sunnehanna Amateur, and had been a member of the 1972 winning American team in the Eisenhower Trophy. That same year he was runner-up in the US Amateur Championship and tied for third place in a US Tour event, the Heritage Classic.

His first round as a professional came on 1 November 1973. It was a 65. Ben followed up with rounds of 72, 66 and 67 and that was good enough to win the Texas Open by two strokes. A few days later his explosive start continued in the World Open, played over a marathon eight rounds, at Pinehurst. He threatened to win that one too, especially after a 64 in the sixth round, but in the end took second place behind Miller Barber.

Had another Nicklaus arrived? The publicity was frantic and the twenty-one-year-old Crenshaw was almost in the superstar bracket. And, just as quickly, out of it, though his name remained in the forefront. He won no tournaments in the next two seasons, but did come desperately close to winning the US Open at Medinah in 1975. Standing on the 71st tee, he held a one-stroke lead over the best finisher at that time, John Mahaffey. He was faced with a 220-yard par-3, played over water. Crenshaw decided on plenty of club and selected a 2-iron. The swing looked good, but he caught the ball on the toe of the club. The ball still almost carried to the green, but fell a yard short of the bank at the far side of the lake. He took 5 and the championship was gone. The memory is a bitter one. He had failed to hit a solid professional shot when it was most needed.

Ben's professionalism had been called into question by this time. He had 'a wristy, college boy swing', what might be called 'an amateur swing' in Britain. The backswing was too long and the wrists too loose at the top. Nothing, of course, would have been said if Ben's early professional successes had continued. Instead, he'd have been copied.

It was undeniably true, however, that Crenshaw's driving was sometimes wild, so much so that it helped him to the unofficial title of the best player of spectacular recovery shots on the US Tour, a reputation you can hardly acquire without being often seen in wild country.

Crenshaw listened to the criticism and probably spent too much time fiddling with his swing, making minor adjustments and desperately trying to make it shorter and tighter. Whatever his play was like through the green, Crenshaw was arguably the best putter, and that's a great equalizer.

In 1976 tournament wins began to come, though he still had only eight US Tour successes at the end of 1983, but had won the 1976 Irish Open also. A major championship continued to elude him, though he found himself in contention more often than other more successful tournament performers. He was second in the Open Championship in both 1978 and 1979, and second in the Masters in 1976 and 1983.

His closest encounter, however, came in the 1979 USPGA Championship. At Oakland Hills, Crenshaw had rounds of 69, 67, 69 and 67. His total of 272 was just one above the championship record, but only good enough to tie with Australian David Graham. Crenshaw had the edge on the first two holes of sudden death, only to be thwarted by outrageous putts by the Australian and lost on the third hole.

When April 1984 came round and with it the Masters, Crenshaw had been in good form. His last round prior to the Masters had been a 67 in the Greater Greensboro Open. That was also Ben's score in the first round of the Masters, a superb round of golf which depended little on his legendary putting and recovery skills. For he hit every green in regulation except the 10th, a very long par-4 of 485 yards, where he holed a six-foot putt to save his par. His score of five under was made on the par-5s. He birdied the 8th, 13th and 15th and had two other birdies, one a 2 at the treacherous 12th, the 155-yard par-3 played over Rae's Creek. He was in the lead by a stroke from Lee Trevino.

On the second day Crenshaw lost a little ground with his even par round of 72. This put him four behind the new leader, Mark Lye, who had added 66 to his first round 69. With Crenshaw on 139 were David Graham and Nick Faldo, while Tom Kite was on 138. Of these five players, only David Graham had proved he could win a major championship; Crenshaw, Kite and perhaps Faldo were overdue for one. No one expected the leader, Mark Lye, to see it through.

On the third day Lye did indeed surrender his lead, but his round of 73 was not a bad one and left him just a stroke adrift of Tom Kite, who had birdied the last hole for his total of 207. Crenshaw, Graham and Faldo were all very much in the hunt, two strokes off the lead of 209 after their third rounds of 70 each. At the end of the day only four strokes covered the leading twelve players. It looked as if this were to be another Masters settled over the final nine holes, perhaps by the water hazards at the 12th, 13th and 15th, as so often before. This time, just one hole was to do it.

Crenshaw scored steadily on the first eight holes. He had all pars except the 2nd and 8th, which he birdied. He now entered a golden streak. At the 9th, 435 yards, he struck a 6-iron to ten feet and holed a teasing sidehill putt. (The 9th had been good to him the day before as well, when he had holed from a greenside bunker.) At the 10th, a par-4, Crenshaw was thirty yards or more from the hole and in a fight for his par over the fast, undulating green. He holed the huge putt and swept into a two-stroke lead.

Afterwards Tom Kite described this putt as a killer blow. I wonder why? True it had put Ben into the lead, but there were many holes still to play. The remark may say something about Kite's character. He's a prodigious money-winner, with about $2½ million amassed on the US Tour by the end of 1985, but he seldom wins

Stop the heavy breathing and put those binoculars away or we'll go straight home!

tournaments, only five victories in twelve seasons up to the end of 1983. He had, however, won the Doral-Eastern a month before.

As if to emphasize my point, Crenshaw immediately dropped a shot on the 11th, a hole which Larry Nelson birdied to draw within a stroke of Crenshaw.

And so to the fatal 12th. As I said earlier, it's only 155 yards and seldom plays as much more than a firm 6-iron. The narrow green, only ten yards deep in the middle, is set at an angle to the tee, slanting away to the right. In front is Rae's Creek, perhaps five yards wide, and then an upslope to the green with a large bunker set in its face. There are two bunkers at the rear of the green, again set into the slope, one quite steep with trees beyond. Players tempted to play safe by over-clubbing will be faced with a sand shot from a downhill lie towards the creek. The answer is to hit the right club the right distance, something today's professionals claim to do within five yards. However, the 12th presents one final and severe problem: swirling winds not felt on the tee catch an iron shot as it rises above the tree level and then it's in the lap of the gods.

Larry Nelson's challenge lost much of its momentum on this hole when he put his tee shot in the creek and went on to take 5. Kite was obviously still very much in it, despite that 'killer blow' – until he destroyed himself at the 12th. His tee shot was always too far right of the flag and found the water. He then pitched to the green, but his ball spun back to within a foot or so of the water. Understandably, he was rather too firm with his next shot, leaving himself little chance of getting the putt. A 6 went down on his card. Perhaps his attitude to the tee shot had been too negative. He said later: 'Club selection on the 12th is total guess-work. You just close your eyes and grab a club.'

Crenshaw played a 6-iron three or four yards short of the hole; his putt caught the edge, spun round and in. That was a swing of four shots between him and Tom Kite, all reminiscent of the 1937 Masters, when the leader at the time, Ralph Guldahl took 5 on the hole while Byron Nelson had a 2 and went on to win. It was on this hole too in 1984 that Tom Weiskopf equalled the record high score for a single hole in any Masters. He took 13, but I doubt if he was really trying after his sixth shot!

Crenshaw by now looked the most likely winner and Kite had definitely gone, together with Nick Faldo and David Graham. But others were making moves. Tom Watson was playing steadily as was Larry Nelson, and both Gil Morgan and David Edwards were to put in strong final rounds of 67 to be there waiting if others stumbled, as Ed Sneed did in 1979 and Curtis Strange in 1985.

At the par-5 13th Crenshaw decided to play safely short of the creek, but followed with none too good a pitch shot. However, his long putt was dead. At the 14th he was left with a long putt with a huge borrow, so fast that he merely nudged his ball to set it on its way. It stopped perhaps twenty feet short, but Ben got that one in to save his par. Phew!

There was a bonus on the 15th. Again, Crenshaw played short of the water and pitched up to about five yards. When he holed the putt he was four strokes in the lead. On the same hole Larry Nelson had no such option. He had to go for the green and aimed a big hook out to the right. His ball swung across from right to left, clattered into the stand, bounced on to the Sarazen Bridge and into the water.

In the end, the only real challenge, a forlorn one, came from Tom Watson, who forced birdies out of the 16th and 18th. After parring the 16th and dropping a shot on the 17th, Crenshaw knew that a one over par-5 on the 400-yard final hole would be good enough – but it still had to be done. Crenshaw, instead, took 4 with a 3-wood, a good 6-iron and a comfortable two putts. His total of 277 left him two strokes clear of Tom Watson, with Gil Morgan and David Edwards a stroke further away. Kite finished with a 75 on 282 as did Mark Lye. Faldo struggled home to a 76 and a tie for fifteenth place on 285. Seven days later Faldo won the Sea Pines Heritage Classic and second again was – who else – Tom Kite. Crenshaw had his first major championship in the bag and, sadly, has hardly been heard from since.

10

Players Who Smile With Style

It could just happen that the US Seniors Tour will overtake the appeal of the main American circuit. Although the idea itself is only a very few years old, the over-fifties are sky-rocketing in popularity. Apart from the Senior Championship, which has a history going back many years, discussions about the possibility of a tour only started in 1979. By 1981 there were still only five events, but the total had risen to a dozen just a year later. In 1985, believe it or not, there were twenty-eight and for 1986 there were more sponsors eager to put up the money for a tournament than dates available.

I could say, 'As usual, a man called Arnold Palmer was responsible.' Just as he breathed new life into the Open Championship and caused the TV golf ratings to soar in America, his presence was very important to over-fifties golf. Palmer still had his faithful army following his play on the main US Tour but, to be honest, they have had little to cheer about for a number of years. Amongst the over-fifties, however, the masses could see their man contend and win again. There were also many other good players – Don January, Miller Barber and Gene Littler, for example, and Billy Casper, a later arrival.

The year of 1985 was particularly dramatic on the Seniors Tour. Australian Peter Thomson, in his prime never an outstanding success in America, became the dominating figure. With nine victories he won about a third of the events, taking his money winnings close to

$400,000, which would have put him in third place on the main US Tour. Perhaps he will never again be quite so dominating because, on 1 November 1985, Gary Player celebrated his fiftieth birthday and won his first Seniors tournament at Boca Cove, Florida, later that month.

So the Seniors Tour unarguably boasts four all-time greats and, in about the same number of years ahead, there may be two more competing, Lee Trevino and Jack Nicklaus. How I wish our own Neil Coles would board a liner (he won't fly) and allow himself a couple of months to settle in. I would be eager to buy a share in his prospects, I can tell you. Indeed, I intended to enter myself until a car smash in 1982 caused injuries whose effects linger on.

In the whole of sport this is a revolutionary field, because a golfer in his fifties, if his nerve remains unimpaired, is *almost* as good a player as he was say twenty years earlier. Of what other sport or game could you say that?

So American spectators can follow the golfing personalities they have admired for as long as twenty-five years. There is undoubtedly a threat to the main US Tour, despite the fact that most golfers are past their very best by their early forties. Their personalities, however, may have become more attractive.

That is one of the problems with *under*-fifties golf. There are just too many clones, unsmiling men, who have emerged, almost identical, at the end of the conveyor belt of American college golf. Some make the effort to make themselves identifiable by what they wear. It may be a white Hogan cap (Jack Renner), plus-twos (Payne Stewart), or a fedora (Gary Hallberg).

But these are just the outer trappings. If the man within lacks colour, they help very little. In the 1984 US Open, however, we did have two men fighting it out who stood out above the crowd, Fuzzy Zoeller and Greg Norman, lacking only what Tom Watson once called 'the charisma that comes from winning major champion-

ships'. Zoeller had won one, the 1979 US Masters –
incidentally the first time he was invited to play – and
five other events on the US Tour. Norman had been an
international star for several years, but had played
relatively little in America. His best achievements, I
would say, were winning the Australian Open and
Australian Masters, the World Matchplay Championship twice and leading money-winner on the European
Tour in 1982. He had won more than thirty events
worldwide, but a major championship was overdue.
Would it ever come?

The US Open was held at Winged Foot at
Mamaroneck in the state of New York, where Bobby
Jones won his third title in 1929, Billy Casper his first in
1959, and Hale Irwin his first in 1974. Jones scored 294,
Casper 282 and Irwin 287. This is one way of saying that
of the several hundreds who had played four rounds of
golf over Winged Foot in these US Opens, not one player
had beaten par. After the 1984 Championship there were
still only two, Frank Urban Zoeller and Gregory John
Norman.

Both made a tidy but quiet start to the championship,
Zoeller with a 71 and Norman a round of 70. This may
well have been very pleasing for Fuzzy, who had a
surprisingly poor record in the US Open. In a US Tour
career which began in 1975 he had qualified to compete
seven times, and had missed the thirty-six-hole cut just
about as often as not, with fifteenth being his best finish.
He came a lowly sixty-second on the year's money list.
The leaders, with rounds of 68, were Mike Donald, Hale
Irwin, Jim Thorpe and Hubert Green, while Seve
Ballesteros, Fred Couples and Curtis Strange were
amongst several just a stroke further away.

Trevino's round of 71 said something about Winged
Foot and its stern finish. He reached the turn in 31, but
took 40 to come home. The last six holes took their toll on
Trevino and many others. The 13th is a long par-3 of 212
yards, and the remaining holes are all par-4s of over 400
yards, the last three being around 450 yards each. Unless

players got a long tee shot away, they were always playing long irons or woods to smallish greens. As the first four holes posed rather similar problems, a score usually comes from holes five to twelve, which include the only two par-4s under 400 yards and both the par-5s. Norman, for instance, in his first round was three under after playing twelve holes, but back to a level par-70 for the round at the end.

More than most the Australian was looking to win, for he had run into a spell of very good form. Two weeks earlier at the Congressional Country Club he had won the Kemper Open in very impressive style after leading from start to finish. After one round he was two strokes in the lead, four after two and then a luxurious seven as he stood on the 1st tee in the final round. No one got close, his nearest pursuer being Mark O'Meara, five behind.

On the second day Greg kept himself well in contention for the US Open with a two under par round of 68, which put him six strokes ahead of the favourite, Tom Watson and five ahead of Jack Nicklaus, also well fancied because of his recent win in his own Memorial Tournament at Muirfield Village. The leader, however, was Hale Irwin, who had won the championship at Winged Foot in 1974. He had a second round of 68, with a grandstand finish of birdies on each of those difficult last three holes.

Irwin, with his pedigree of two victories in the US Open, looked the most likely winner, though the round of the day had come from Fuzzy Zoeller, a 66 where he was on every green except one in regulation figures. His game seemed to me very much on song with a consistent draw on his tee shots, the irons flying at the flag and his putting stroke beautifully fluent. Zoeller, however, in his 1979 US Masters victory, had found himself in a play-off with Ed Sneed and Tom Watson when he had never really been in contention. How would he deal with the pressure of being in a potentially winning position early on, his total of 137 for the thirty-six holes being just a stroke worse than Hale Irwin?

Pretty well was the answer. The next day, Zoeller was out last with Irwin, a classic matchplay situation. The championship lead swung to and fro. Zoeller was first in the lead on the 8th, when he holed a long swinging putt from the back of the green for a birdie. Irwin hit back shortly after, only to see Zoeller ahead again with another birdie at the 12th. On the next Irwin levelled with a birdie 2, but Zoeller holed a chip shot on the very next hole. So they went on, with Fuzzy Zoeller usually holding a slight advantage until he faltered on the last two holes, being bunkered near the green on each. This was the position after the third round:

Irwin	205
Zoeller	206
Norman	207
Thorpe	209

Zoeller, Irwin and Norman were round in 69, Thorpe a stroke more and the stage was set for another matchplay bout between Irwin and Zoeller, with Norman ready to intervene. It didn't seem to me that Thorpe, a powerful but unsubtle player, had quite the quality to feature at the finish. So it was to prove. Thorpe's final round of 73 just wasn't good enough.

But the match between the two Americans didn't come off either. You may remember that Irwin had 78 to finish the 1979 British Open Championship, when he had looked the most likely winner. Even when winning his second US Open title earlier that year, he had played a distinctly rocky last nine holes. On that occasion, however, his lead had been almost unassailable.

I'm not saying that Irwin cracked on any of these occasions. It's very easy to trot out glibly such a remark when a man in contention produces a relatively poor final round. We should remember that he may simply have been a little off his game on the day. Golfers aren't automatons for there's such a narrow margin between a crisp iron shot and a poor one or the putt that just topples in and the one which doesn't.

Irwin and Zoeller exchanged shots on the first two holes of the final round, which left Irwin still with his one-stroke lead. There came a big swing on the 3rd, however, where Fuzzy sank a good putt for his birdie 2 to Irwin's 4. Zoeller was ahead and then went on to birdie the next three holes, the sort of burst that can easily win a championship, especially if the pursuers become discouraged.

By the end of the first nine, Irwin was surely gone, out in 40 to Zoeller's 32. So it was to prove for he did little better on the second nine to finish with 79 for sixth place. Only about half a dozen of the sixty-three players who qualified to play the final day scored worse than that.

Soon it seemed that Greg Norman would be the main challenger, yet a birdie from the Australian on the 7th did no more than pull him to within three strokes of the man who seemed to be running away with the championship. The 14th, however, was a very significant hole. Norman played it to perfection, hitting his approach shot a few yards past the hole and then holing the putt, gaining two strokes on the American, who pulled his tee shot into deep rough and eventually took 5. With four holes to go, the battle was on, Zoeller's lead cut to a single stroke.

After both had parred the 15th, that stretch of three par-4s around 450 yards was all that remained. At the 16th, Norman saved his par by getting down in two when his second shot finished halfway down a bank at the side of the green. He needed a deft cut-up shot and holed a good putt. Zoeller had to follow with a saving shot of his own. With too much hook on his tee shot, his direct line to the green was blocked out by trees. However, taking a 3-iron, he managed to draw his shot around the trees and saw it pitch short of the green and run on. With that crisis passed, he then hit a fine drive to the 17th where Norman was already in trouble ahead. The Australian sent his tee shot to the right into trees, and from there had no shot except just to pitch his ball back to the fairway. From there, with 160 yards still to go, he hit his

6-iron just two or three yards from the hole and got the putt to save his par. That closed the gap. For Zoeller was bunkered short of the green and took three more to get down.

What a performance followed from Norman on the 18th. He began with a very long drive that left him a 6-iron to the green. Contenders really shouldn't miss a green with this club, which is just about the easiest in the bag. Norman didn't just miss the green, however. He hit a terrible shot, way right into a grandstand where it was caught by a spectator who did the decent thing and handed it back to the Australian when he arrived at the scene of the crime.

After he had taken his free drop, Greg faced a difficult pitch. His ball was well down in the rough and with the green well above him. He could just see the top of the flag. Norman was too firm, pitching through the green and leaving himself a putt of forty feet or more from a collar of rough.

Later, Norman was to say that he could see the line of the putt immediately and had a nice feel of the pace in his hands. All well and good but they usually miss from that distance, especially as there were about four feet of borrow. But Greg set his ball off on the chosen line. It followed the contours of the green and coasted down and into the hole. Three holes played; three pars saved.

Back down the fairway Zoeller waited to play. A great roar went up and Greg raised his arms on high. Zoeller thought it was a birdie putt, giving the Australian a one-stroke lead. He walked over to his bag, took his towel and waved it aloft as a gesture of surrender. Norman smiled and acknowledged.

Zoeller soon learned that the putt had been for par and matched it safely. The next day saw the first US Open play-off since Medinah in 1975, when Lou Graham and John Mahaffey were the players involved. I wonder if this will be the last over eighteen holes. The US PGA has been sudden death for several years and so has the Masters. The R and A decreed a rather less sudden death form for the 1985 Open Championship, but the eighteen-hole play-off has presumably gone for ever.

The play-off between Zoeller and Norman was an anti-climax, yet the beginning had the ingredients of high drama, with Zoeller holing a good-length putt for a birdie and Norman following him into the hole from not much closer. In retrospect, the 2nd hole more or less settled the title. Norman drove into the rough and his third shot was about eight yards from the hole. Fuzzy Zoeller then coasted a huge downhill putt – say twenty yards – into the hole for his birdie 3. Perhaps shaken, Greg three-putted and was suddenly three strokes behind the American, not an easy margin to make up, even with sixteen holes still to go.

He showed few signs of doing so. On the next hole, with Zoeller on his way to a bogey, Norman had an immediate chance to get a stroke back – but three-putted once again. When he dropped another shot on the 4th, the contest was beginning to look more like a procession. Of course, it's always possible to make up a deficit of six or seven shots in strokeplay. It just isn't very likely, especially as one man's confidence grows and the other becomes increasingly desperate to strike a telling blow. At the end Zoeller was round in 67 and Norman in 75. Both had played smiling, friendly golf and how glad I was to see it.

11

Trevino's Last Fling?

Outside the ranks of a few great players, most top-class performers begin to peak in their mid-twenties and manage to keep it going for ten years or so. Lee Buck Trevino won his fifth major championship, the US PGA of 1974, in his mid-thirties. His results continued to be good over the next few years, especially in 1980, when he won three US Tour events, the Vardon Trophy for the year's low-stroke average and was second in the money list.

As he got further into his forties, Trevino's standards fell away quite sharply. He seemed to be concentrating more on promotion and TV work, and playing rather more overseas where he could command large appearance money. Surely his days as a real major championship contender were over.

All this was to change dramatically with the 1984 US PGA Championship, played at Shoal Creek, Alabama, a Jack Nicklaus-designed course. Trevino had more or less completed his TV work for the year and had been playing some tournament golf. In July he had played in the Open Championship at St Andrews, and at the halfway stage was tied for second place with Nick Faldo and Seve Ballesteros, three strokes behind the unlikely leader, Australian Ian Baker-Finch. For Trevino, that was more or less that. Putting poorly he trailed away, after opening rounds of 70 and 67, to 75 and 73.

About a month later, however, he played well in the Buick Open and tied for fourth place, three strokes behind the winner, South African Denis Watson. Trevino had a remarkable 64 in his second round.

The reason was a new putter. Lee had noted that almost all the high finishers at St Andrews had used PINGs, so when he got to Rosendaelsche at Arnhem for the Dutch Open Championship, he went into the professional's shop to make his choice amongst what might be on offer. There was just one. Lee took it, even though the club was too upright for his putting stroke and had too much loft on the face. Did he make his requirements known and leave it to the PING company to make adjustments? Not a bit of it. He simply took it back to his hotel and banged it and stamped on it until he had it finely tuned. Trevino then went out and played very well in the championship, finishing in a tie for third place, but five strokes behind Bernhard Langer.

On his way to Shoal Creek for the PGA Championship, Trevino was encouraged by the thought that it was a Bermuda grass course. He knew he had a few tricks up his sleeve, and the experience of knowing that divots are more shallow and iron shots tend to fly some ten yards or so further. At 7145 yards it was a long course, and Trevino as a driver of the ball has always been 'long enough' but not long. His usually reliable fade, however, does enable him to stay on most fairways. That was to prove vital, for the ball settled well down in the semi-rough, often making any kind of long shot out of the question.

Trevino began well with a 69, three under par, which put him in a tie for second place, one stroke behind Lanny Wadkins, Raymond Floyd and Mike Reid (another player noted for his ability to keep the ball in play).

The story of the second day was Gary Player's round. Here was a man who had seemed to be marking time, waiting to qualify to play on the US Senior Tour. Well, he went round Shoal Creek in 63, a record for the PGA Championship, and at the end of play was tied for the lead with Lanny Wadkins and, yes, Lee Trevino, who had gone round in 68.

It was Trevino who almost wrapped up the event in

his third round, producing scoring in the Player class. Over the first seven holes he had four birdies and an eagle. When he went on to birdie the 11th, he had opened up a four-stroke lead on his closest pursuer, at this time Lanny Wadkins. He followed with six pars and seemed assured of a commanding lead going into the final round when he came to the last tee, a round of 65 in sight. He had to hit the fairway first, something he hadn't done in the previous two rounds. This time he was bunkered on the right but decided to go for the green with a 6-iron, risky with water protecting most of the green. He pulled his shot and had to take the medicine. Even with a 6 on the last, he was still round in 67. It wasn't as bad as what had happened to Nick Faldo earlier. He had been well placed with his second round almost completed, but had taken 8 on this hole. With that, his chances of winning the championship were virtually over.

Trevino went into the final round with his best opportunity to add to his five major championships for years. At twelve under par he held a one-stroke lead over Lanny Wadkins and was two better than the rejuvenated Gary Player. However, his lead was a thin one. It could disappear in the first minutes of the final round, in which these three were out last. Playing together, the odds were surely that the thirty-four-year-old Wadkins would stand the pressure far better than either of the two much older men.

If championships and tournaments are almost always settled over the last nine holes, a good start is still essential. Many a contender fades right away after dropping shots early on. Trevino's start was very good: he birdied the 1st. Although Trevino declared he wasn't nervous, it was a great boost to his confidence. A three-putt start could have destroyed him there and then.

Trevino was in his first real trouble on the 6th, a par-5. With his second shot threatened by a creek he went for the green, and cleared the water but found a bunker. His next shot was through the green, settling in thickish rough. When Wadkins birdied the hole, the pair were level at thirteen under par. Tommy Nakajima and Player were three behind, and Ballesteros began to close up when he birdied both the 9th and 10th holes to go to ten under.

On the 9th Player made his bid to win a tenth major championship and his third PGA. He holed a putt of absurd length which brought roars from the crowd and even a little laughter. For it was so improbable. Let's settle for calling it a thirty-five-yarder. The hole was also very significant for the other main contenders. Wadkins holed from about five yards for a birdie, which took him into a one-stroke lead, and Trevino saved himself by getting down in two from a bunker.

As suddenly as Gary had put himself into contention, he fell away again. Faced with a medium-length putt for a birdie on the 10th, he stroked his ball tentatively and ended up seven feet short. It seemed inevitable that he'd miss and he did, falling three behind the leader.

Each hole was now a drama. On the 11th Trevino drove into the trees, but managed to save his par with a good putt. Wadkins was also in trouble from the tee and had to play a long iron third shot to the green and found a bunker. When he failed to get down in two, the pair were level once more. On the 13th Wadkins handed over the lead by taking three putts.

At this point the position was: Trevino −13, Wadkins −12, followed at −11 by a new man, Calvin Peete, who was playing one of the best rounds of the final day but couldn't get many putts to drop. Tied at −10 were Gary Player and Seve Ballesteros, trying all he knew to put in a last round charge and add another major to his recent Open Championship victory at St Andrews.

At the 14th Trevino went two ahead of Wadkins when he birdied the hole, as did Gary Player. At the next, however, with both men only about a yard from the hole, Trevino missed and Wadkins didn't, reducing the gap to only one stroke.

The last three holes at Shoal Creek play to a par of 3, 5

and 4. Wadkins made his last real move on the par-3, ripping in an iron shot to about eight feet. Trevino was bunkered, with little green between him and the flag. He could get no closer than about four yards. As he prepared to putt there was the prospect of his taking a 4 and Wadkins a birdie 2 to lead by one. But it didn't work out like that. Trevino got his putt and Wadkins didn't.

At the par-5 17th, Lanny Wadkins knew he had to get home in two to wipe out the one-stroke lead. With the honour, he hooked into the rough, while Trevino found the fairway. Striving for length Wadkins made poor contact with his ball and got little distance. He couldn't hope to reach the green in three, which Trevino did comfortably, eventually making 5 to Wadkins' 6.

Trevino was delighted to take a two-stroke lead into the final hole. After all, he'd taken 6 the last time he'd played it and hadn't hit the fairway all week. This time he did. With that tee shot, the championship was almost certainly his. The final moment of drama had nothing to do with winning and losing but just statistics. Trevino's second shot with a 7-iron came to rest some half a dozen yards from the hole. With Wadkins taking 5 and the rest of the field out of it, Trevino could have afforded four putts. Instead, he did it in one, his ball spinning round the hole before it toppled in. He had won by four strokes and that single putt gave him a round of 69 and the distinction of being one of the very few players who have won a major championship with four rounds under 70, just as he'd been the first to accomplish the feat in the 1968 US Open Championship. This time his scores were 69, 68, 67, 69 for a 273 total.

The ages of the first four past the post are interesting:

First   Trevino (fourty-four)
Second   Wadkins (thirty-four) and Player (forty-eight)
Fourth   Peete (forty-one)

Just three men older than Trevino have won a major championship – Julius Boros was forty-eight when he won the 1968 US PGA Championship, Old Tom Morris forty-six when he took the Open Championship of 1867, as was Jack Nicklaus on winning the 1986 Masters. Roberto de Vicenzo and Harry Vardon were also forty-four when they won Open Championships, but both were several months younger than Trevino.

12

A Battle for Supremacy

In all the long history of golf, there hasn't been much argument about who is or was the leading golfer of the day. The greatest players have always been men who could pull out that vital something extra when the pressure was highest and the prize the greatest.

Since the Second World War, they've come and gone: Byron Nelson, Ben Hogan, Arnold Palmer and Jack Nicklaus. In Nicklaus' case, rivals appeared from time to time – Lee Trevino, Tom Weiskopf and Johnny Miller, for example – but each proved to be a threat to his pre-eminence that quickly faded. Jack remained the unquestioned number one, until Tom Watson came along and established himself as one of the greatest players from 1975 onwards.

For a while, both of them reigned as the 'Big Two', a position which was typified by their great thirty-six-hole duel in the Turnberry Open Championship of 1977. When it seemed that Nicklaus, after a very bad year indeed in 1979, had finally been toppled by Watson, back he came to the very top with two major championship victories in 1980. There were some who asked in all seriousness if Jack could go on for ever, or at least until he was fifty.

Despite his great 1986 Masters victory I think the answer to that question will be no. 1980 saw his final flowering. Tom Watson became the world's leading player, even if he had been unacknowledged from about 1977.

But not for long. A challenger had arisen from the Bay of Santander in northern Spain, his name Severiano Ballesteros, the first European to become the best player in the world since those far-off days before the First World War when James Braid, John Henry Taylor and Harry Vardon carried all before them.

Ballesteros was almost immediately recognized as a great talent when, as a complete unknown, he swash-buckled his way to a second-place finish in the 1976 Open Championship at Royal Birkdale and went on to a sequence of tournament wins. Those victories proved he was no shooting star to enjoy his brief headlines, then vanish from the stage. Soon the major championships began to come his way, first the 1979 British Open Championship at Royal Lytham and St Anne's. It caused a few leading American players to scoff at his wayward driving, and claim he'd won because the rough had been well trampled and his sand iron and putter had been working exceptionally well. They should have been convinced by Seve's performance in the 1980 US Masters. This time wayward shots were rare. This was a tournament Ballesteros took by the scruff of the neck, only stumbling a little in the final round when perhaps his thoughts were on breaking the record or what to say in his victory speech. However, after the stumbles he wasn't consumed by fears of losing, like Ed Sneed the previous year or Curtis Strange in 1985. As the field closed up, Ballesteros regained his composure. Seven strokes ahead going into the final round, he cruised in comfortably with a four-stroke margin over Gibby Gilbert and Jack Newton, with the big guns, Tom Watson and Jack Nicklaus, nine and sixteen strokes in his wake.

Many players have one major championship to their name; far fewer a second. Ballesteros was on the march. But the general level of play today is higher than it was in the days of Hagen, Jones and, yes, even Hogan and the early Nicklaus. Today anyone amongst the masses of good players can win when suddenly it seems easy to drive straight and the line and strength of every putt is obvious. So Seve didn't continue to pile on the major championships as the great players of bygone years had done. Such achievements are more unlikely today. Even so, like Tom Watson, Jack Nicklaus or Bobby Jones he has that very extra special something which enables them to be sharper of strike and stronger of will on the great occasions. They always seem to be in contention, even when in poor form.

Going into the 1980s, Tom Watson was emphatically number one, with a Masters title and five wins in the Open Championship between 1975 and 1983. The seal was probably set on his career by that little lob shot on the 71st hole at Pebble Beach in 1982 which went into the hole and gave him his first US Open Championship victory.

But there's an end to all things. Ben Hogan, after winning three majors in 1953, was obviously going to pick up a few more in the years ahead. Yet he won nothing else of real note. In 1980 Nicklaus had re-established himself as the best there was. Arnold Palmer played consummate golf in the 1962 Open Championship at Troon and the 1964 US Masters so that many were speculating about chances of his overhauling Bobby Jones's record, which had stood since 1930, of thirteen major championship victories.

In each of these cases, and with apologies to Jack Nicklaus, history has shown that their day was over.

Frankly, in the case of Thomas Sturges Watson, my crystal ball doesn't reveal what will happen. In 1985 he had a very poor year by his own standards, with ominous doubts concerning his putting stroke being heard for the first time. Tom will, however, remain a leading player in the years to come. He may well win more tournaments and championships, but as the best golf player in the world, he was overtaken by Severiano Ballesteros in 1982 and 1983. The difference between the two was made very clear in 1985, when Seve won six times and Watson not one.

It all began with the 1983 US Masters at Augusta

National, Georgia, a course that suits both players. Great length from the tee is a huge advantage and so is a silky touch on the glassy undulating greens. Both are suitably endowed. Both can also play a draw from the tee which is most helpful at Augusta. The battle for supremacy was on and over a course that suited their talents as well as any. Both are long hitters and fly the ball high, have excellent judgement of pace and line in long putting and are resolute at holing out.

After the first round, played out in cloudy weather with rain causing a forty-minute suspension of play, the leaders were almost all names well known to the golfing public: with 67s, there were Gil Morgan, Raymond Floyd and Jack Renner; a stroke behind were Charles Coody, the 1971 Champion, a young amateur called James Hallett, J. C. Snead, nephew of the great Sam, Arnold Palmer enjoying his moment of glory and Severiano Ballesteros. Tom Watson was handily placed, three strokes behind the lead.

The second day's play, Friday, was completely washed out by rain and not every player had completed his second round on the Saturday when play was called off for the day. Morgan moved into the lead, his round of 70 giving him a total of 137. Close behind came:

Ballesteros   (68, 70) 138
Floyd   (67, 72) and Keith Fergus (70, 69) 139
Nick Faldo   (70, 70) and Jodie Mudd (72, 68) 140

Tom Watson was one stroke further behind, together with defending champion Craig Stadler. Even if the weather improved, there would have to be a Monday finish.

In the third round, Ballesteros' driving was both long and accurate, but his iron play was sub-standard and he missed a couple of short putts. However, a good putt on the last green from about four yards for a birdie improved the look of his card and he was round in 73. By contrast Ray Floyd had a look of infallibility on the short putts and Stadler, helped by some good scrambling, also

120

improved his position. With a round to play it was still a wide-open contest:

Floyd, Stadler   210
Ballesteros   211
Watson, Mudd   212

By a quirk of statistics, Seve had been a stroke behind the changing leadership after each round, a very handy place to be. The player avoids the extra pressure of being the leader yet the adrenalin of contending is in full flow.

Ballesteros wrote the central story of the 1983 US Masters during the first hour of his final round. The first four holes at Augusta are a 400-yard par 4, a 555-yard par-5, another par-4 of 360 yards and then a 200-yard par-3. Ballesteros began with one of the most irresistible bursts ever seen at this stage of a major championship – birdie, eagle, par, birdie. Four holes played and four under par for the round. Those minutes meant that he needed only par golf for the rest of his round to be sure of victory – unless some other player could produce a comparable spell of turbo-charged golf.

In the event the overnight leaders, Stadler and Floyd, seemed shaken. To see the unbelievable changes on the leader board caused by the man out a few minutes ahead of you bewilders the mind. Ballesteros reached the turn in 31, just one more than the record set by Johnny Miller in 1975, then birdied the difficult 10th hole. At this point, Floyd and Stadler trailed by four strokes. Later, on the two par-5s, eagle chances for both, were squandered. By then their hopes were spent. Faced with that opening burst, it must have been difficult not to throw in the towel and decide that the fates had decreed this was the Spaniard's championship. Stadler finished with a round of 76 and tied for sixth place. Floyd's 75 gave him a share of fourth. Two men with no real hope of winning, Ben Crenshaw and Tom Kite, had rounds of 68 and 69 and tied for second place.

Just one man made a tussle of it: Tom Watson, who was paired with Ballesteros. For a while he was the only

real threat to the Spaniard, and only three strokes behind him as they played the 14th, a par-4 of just over 400 yards. Here Watson hit his second shot heavily and then was too strong with his third. He needed to be down with a chip and a single putt for a bogey, but missed from four feet. That was more or less that. Watson hooked from the next tee; Ballesteros was very long and straight and allowed himself the luxury of laying up short of the water hazard at this par-5. Then, at the par-3 16th, he showed his touch and nerve on the long putts when he coasted a long one stone dead.

There remained the drama of the 18th, which has become a small part of the growing Ballesteros legend. He needed only to play this par-4 in 7 to win and began by cutting his tee shot into the trees, but his ball luckily came out onto the fairway again. Seve followed with far too strong an approach shot, perhaps 20 yards through the green and close to the scorer's tent.

From there Ballesteros was faced with a very difficult shot. It was easy enough to be too strong and run through the green or into a bunker. With those thoughts in mind, his chip was underhit and ended up short of the green. For a few moments there was a possibility of disaster, if say Seve thinned his next one into a bunker and then and then . . . He stopped such idle speculation by chipping his next shot into the hole for a par-4, a 69, a total of 280 and victory by four strokes.

Shortly afterwards, Ballesteros made himself unpopular with the American golf authorities by announcing that although his victory qualified him for the Tournament of Champions, he had promised to play in the far less prestigious Madrid Open in Spain. In fact, he continued, having played six times in America that year, he intended to play in only three more events, the Westchester Classic and the two remaining major championships, the US Open and PGA.

Ballesteros departed for Spain, where he gave an exhibition at Real Madrid's Barnabeu Stadium and competed in the Madrid Open, as he had declared he would, watched by King Juan Carlos.

By the time he came back to America a couple of months later, he had lost a play-off for the Italian Open to Bernhard Langer, having finished with a birdie and an eagle for a 66 to get into it, but shortly after won the PGA Championship at the end of May at Royal St George's, Sandwich, where he had taken 84 on his first outing back in 1975.

Some ten days later came the Westchester Classic, a warm-up event for Ballesteros before the US Open and a renewal of his duel with Tom Watson. With an eagle on the last hole, he won it.

For the US Open at Oakmont Country Club in Pennsylvania, Ballesteros was confronted with what he thought the toughest course he had ever played. The greens were a particularly frightening pace. One American professional was heard to remark that when he marked his ball with a dime it slid off the green. The United States Golf Association officials, even if not believing this tale, decided they were indeed a little on the fast side even though pace is what they want for the US Open. The tool they use for testing the speed is called a Stimpmeter. It's set up on a flat piece of green and a ball is released from the device. At Oakmont readings of fourteen feet of roll were possible as against something of the order of eleven feet at Augusta for the Masters. You would expect around eight feet on quick greens in Britain. The delicacy of touch required at Oakmont was just too extreme, so the greens were watered to take out some of the sting.

There was no question, however, of making the rough any easier. It is sometimes watered and fertilized to ensure dense growth but a wet spring and high temperatures in the run-up to the Open made this unnecessary. It was extremely penal, causing Ballesteros, and many others, to leave the driver and 3-wood in the bag for most tee shots to the par-4s and 5s.

As expected, scoring was high throughout the championship, a score of 151 after two rounds being good enough to beat the cut-off point. After the first round, the lead was held by Ballesteros, John Mahaffey and Bob Murphy with 69s. It is some indication of the difficulties of Oakmont that two of these were to finish virtually nowhere. Murphy followed with 81 and in the end finished twenty-two strokes behind the champion, while Mahaffey was still tied for the lead after two rounds but then soared to final rounds of 79 and 78 to finish in thirty-fourth place. And both of these are very experienced campaigners.

After two rounds, this was the position:

Mahaffey and Joey Rassett   141
Tom Watson and Ray Floyd   142

Of these four, only Watson was to survive the championship without a poor round. Ballesteros had faltered, with 74. Even so, this was better than par for the field and he lay handily placed on 143, the clear favourite with Watson.

On Saturday Larry Nelson turned the championship on its head and proved that it was possible to produce a low score. His 65 was one of the most remarkable rounds ever played. At the 5th, following rounds of 75 and 73, he was seven over par for the championship and then played the remaining fourteen holes so well that he was back to level par for the championship.

To put that score in perspective, there were just eighteen rounds under 70 in the whole championship, just three better than 69 and two under 68, both played by Larry Nelson. He set a record for the last two rounds of a US Open on a course that was just a little too difficult for the modern professional. However, it was thought that Nelson would not come close to equalling his third-round 65 in his final round.

Watson and Ballesteros were the men to watch. They too had good third rounds, 70 for Watson and 69 for the Spaniard. They held the lead:

Watson and Ballesteros   212
Nelson and Calvin Peete   213

Floyd   214
Gil Morgan   215
Hal Sutton and Andy North   216

Ballesteros had been unable to catch Tom Watson most of the way through the round, but his finish was impressive. It began with a magnificent 3-iron to just a couple of yards at the 15th for a birdie, and both players then birdied the 17th. Seve finally drew level on the last hole with a safe par while Watson, though only a very few feet off the fairway with his tee shot, felt he could attempt nothing more than a sand iron to get his ball back in play. That was a shot gone.

The final round was reminiscent of the Masters a couple of months before. This time, however, it was Watson who had all the inspiration. He began with four birdies on the first six holes, was three strokes ahead by the 8th and reached the turn in 31, the same score and much the same start as Seve had produced at Augusta. The reigning US Open Champion looked certain to win and his every movement was crisp and confident.

It was clear that Ballesteros couldn't win, but the man who lay ninety-second on the US money list and had a major championship to his credit, the 1981 PGA, was still in with much more than a shout. Larry Nelson was playing just about as convincingly as in his 65 the previous day. He had three birdies in the first seven holes and got to the turn in 33, still behind Watson but he caught him at last with a birdie at the 14th. At this point the rains came and it wasn't long before the course was under water. Play was suspended with only six players still to complete their rounds and an hour or so later abandoned until Monday morning. What a time to have to call a halt, the closest to the finish in my experience.

At 10 a.m. on the Monday, Watson began with an approach putt at the 14th, while Nelson hit a 4-wood to the par-3 16th. It was on the green but on the top level, some twenty yards or more from the hole. Could Nelson avoid three-putting? He did better than he could have dreamed, holing that monster putt. It was indeed a

championship-winning shot except this was a championship many said Watson lost. At the 18th Nelson took
three putts. This left Watson having to par the last two
holes to earn a play-off. His chance really went on the
17th, where he bunkered his approach shot, came out
close to the pin but then missed a fairly short putt. He
never threatened to birdie the last, hitting a 7-iron
through the green. He had lost to Nelson, but finished
five strokes ahead of Ballesteros.

The next round in a contest for supremacy that neither
Ballesteros or Watson would admit existed went even
more emphatically to the American. This was the 1983
Open Championship at Royal Birkdale. After thirty-six
holes, Watson had rounds of 67 (which included a
penalty stroke) and 68, which left Seve seven strokes
behind and his third round of 69 only reduced the deficit
to six. He was never at the forefront of this championship, and even a fine last round of 68 did no more than
pull him up into a tie for sixth place, four strokes behind
Tom's 275, which won Watson his fifth Open Championship.

When both finished well down the field in the US
PGA, the year, as regards the major championships, had
gone to Watson rather than Seve. Both had won once,
but Tom had twice been in contention over the final nine
holes while Seve had not. Their placings were:

Watson T-Fourth, Second, First, T-Forty-seventh
Ballesteros First, T-Fourth, T-Sixth, T-Twenty-
seventh

Overall, however, it was far more Seve's year. He
won twice in America, three times in Europe and ended
his season by winning the Sun City Challenge in
Bophuthatswana. Against that, there was Watson's sole
victory in the Open Championship. There had been no
more duels between the two. After all, they are seldom
both in the same field except in the major championships
and there are far fewer US Tour events, where both have
a limited schedule, than you might think.

Apart from his Open Championship victory, 1983 was Watson's worst year since he became a great player. In the years 1977 to 1982, he had been leading US money-winner four times and third and fifth in the other two years. It was quite a slip to finish twelfth and his winnings of $200,000 plus have become commonplace in America. However, Watson began 1984 with a bang, winning the Seiko Matchplay Championship at Tucson at the beginning of January. He went on to have a very good year in America. Once again he was leading money-winner at the end with close on half a million dollars, and was acclaimed the US Tour Player of the Year for the sixth time (incidentally one more than Jack Nicklaus' total).

In America Ballesteros played fifteen times to Watson's twenty but his best performances were a couple of third places to Watson's three wins, two seconds and a third. The Spaniard won little more than a quarter of Watson's money total. Yet the European Press and radio and TV commentators tended to rate Seve as the world number one, a status few would have accorded him in America. Though his abilities have long been recognized there, it is perhaps with some reluctance.

The reason for this difference is the high status we give the Open Championship. What a dramatic one it was in 1984, exciting all through and seldom matched over the climactic final holes.

As is almost a habit with reigning Masters champions, Ballesteros failed to make the thirty-six-hole cut in April and had to ponder his failure for two days while he waited to perform his remaining task – helping the new champion into the traditional green jacket. The man inside it was Ben Crenshaw. It was no hardship. The Open Championship is the Spaniard's greatest love, the Masters comes second. Watson, with a spurt towards the end, came second. Two months later, and neither featured strongly in the US Open, with Seve fading out over the final thirty-six holes.

He had not been playing well in America, but a tip

during practice rounds before the Open Championship at St Andrews worked wonders. Equally important was the fact that he was back in a land where he is accorded honorary British nationality by spectators. They love the Spaniard, but only respect Watson.

Seve began with a round of professional competence rather than brilliance, the dazzle coming with his scoring around the loop. From the 8th to the 12th, he had five 3s consecutively and his only really poor play came on the feared Road hole, the 17th. He hit his tee shot well left, then pulled his second shot. Trying a run-up third shot he was not quite firm enough and still short of the green. He got his 5, however, which is perhaps the real par for this 461-yard hole. That first day, there were just three 3s, thirty-six par-4s and the remaining 117 in the field had 5s or worse.

Watson played very steadily, his long putting looking particularly secure. Again and again he ran the ball at the hole at just the right pace, but nothing dropped for him. He was over par just once at (where else?) the 17th. For the record, the actual leaders were:

Bill Longmuir, Greg Norman and Peter Jacobsen   67
Ian Baker-Finch   68
Ballesteros, Tom Kite, Nick Faldo and Jaime Gonzalez   69

On the second day, the little-known Australian Baker-Finch made much more impact. Beginning at four under par, he moved to a remarkable ten under after ten holes. He kept going to the end, even parring the 17th, for a round of 66 and a three-stroke lead.

The 17th was very much a feature of both Watson's and Ballesteros' rounds as well. Seve found his second shot on the downslope at the rear of the Road bunker and failed to get out, perhaps through being over-ambitiously delicate, but his fourth shot was four feet from the hole. He got the putt.

Playing behind, Watson needed pars on the last three

holes for a round of 66. He got his 4 on the 16th safely enough, but then bunkered his second shot at the 17th, recovered to the front right of the green and left his approach putt eight or nine feet short and missed it. When he parred the last, he had the same round as the Spaniard, a 68. This was the position:

Baker-Finch   134
Faldo, Ballesteros and Trevino   137
Longmuir   138
Wadkins, Couples, Langer and Watson   139

It was easy enough to scoff at the real chances of the twenty-three-year-old Australian, but a young player has to arrive some time. Few had heard of Walter Hagen or Gene Sarazen before they won their first US Opens or Taylor and Vardon before their first Open Championship victories. However, it certainly seemed more significant that the two favourites, Watson and Ballesteros, were in good command of their games.

Tom, in fact, played the best round of the third day of those in the contention. His 66 was matched only by Sam Torrance and an American not qualified to play on the US Tour, Bill Bergin. Watson was in full and glorious flow. He did drop a shot on the 2nd hole, but with five birdies reached the turn in 32 and then drove to five or so yards of the hole on the 342-yard 10th for another birdie. Another followed at the 12th, and par followed par until he reached the 17th, which might again turn a 66 into a 68. This time he showed a way to play the hole that made its problems seem relatively simple. He hit his tee shot down the left half of the fairway, and played for the front of the green rather than the flag. His very long approach putt was stone dead.

Ballesteros was out with Lee Trevino, whose efforts were frustrated by relatively poor putting. Although this certainly didn't apply to Ballesteros, he was gaining very little on the greens but was consistent in everything else he attempted. There was one exception. He hit an atrocious iron to the 178-yard 8th hole, finishing left and in heather some thirty to forty yards short. A superb recovery shot made his putt for a par a formality. On the 17th he took his third successive 5. After three rounds, he had been over par only four times. Three of those bogeys came on the 17th, where Watson had fared no better with 5, 6, and his 4 in the third round.

By this time the championship had all the makings of a four-horse race:

Watson and Baker-Finch	205
Ballesteros and Langer	207

The next men, Hugh Baiocchi, Lanny Wadkins and Lee Trevino were five strokes further away on 212.

On the final day the horses were quickly reduced to three. Baker-Finch's pitch to the 1st unluckily spun back into the burn and he took a bogey 5. Another bogey followed on the 4th, with a further two shots dropped on the 6th and yet another on the 7th. He dropped four more shots in his round, but a birdie on the last enabled him to break 80.

Two of the other three did not come through the opening holes unharmed. Watson, looking far less convincing than in his previous two rounds, dropped shots at the 2nd and 4th but repaired some of the damage with a birdie on the 3rd. Langer, after starting with a pitch to about one foot on the 1st, dropped shots on the 3rd and 5th. Ballesteros went on his steady way with 4 after 4. At the end, there were a remarkable sixteen on his card. He had 4s on both the par-5s and one of the two par-3s.

His play throughout was in great contrast to his championship win at Royal Lytham in 1979 where some of his drives were quite wild. Afterwards, Seve explained that at Lytham he had driven into the rough deliberately, to avoid bunkers or secure the best line in to the flag. Hm, well perhaps. This time he claimed his main aim from the tee was to avoid the eccentric bunkering of St Andrews, and I often saw him well over to the left side of the course. However, on the Old Course a tee shot down the right almost invariably gives the best line in for the second shot, so Seve was demanding a great deal from his short game and it didn't fail him.

Watson gave up his lead on the 12th, a hole just over 300 yards and one of the easiest birdie opportunities you'll find at St Andrews. Watson drove into bracken on the left and had to drop out under penalty, taking a very unwelcome 5. However, he came back minutes later with a birdie at the 13th. On the long 14th Ballesteros' drive just missed the Beardie bunkers. He seemed to take this as an omen of victory and, as at Lytham five years earlier, almost broke into a run in his haste to get to his ball and hit it again. Some hit this one was, a carry of some 240 yards over Hell bunker. He made it but was still some seventy yards from the hole, ran it up to twelve feet and holed the putt to draw level again with Watson. His partner Langer also had a birdie putt, but missed and fell two behind the leaders. It was 5 o'clock exactly.

Langer was to finish his round courageously, taking the brave line with his tee shots on both the 16th and 17th: down the right side of the fairway, risking going out of bounds because of a better line in to the flag and the birdies he desperately needed. Alas, they didn't come. He had to wait until the 18th, where he got his 3 – but too late.

Both Watson and Ballesteros parred the 15th and 16th, the Spaniard only a bare quarter inch away from a birdie on the 16th. A play-off now seemed by far the most likely result. I expected both to drop a shot on the daunting Road hole and perhaps have birdie chances on the 'easy' 18th (no hole is easy when a championship is within reach).

On the Road hole, Seve's record in the previous rounds was 5, 5, 5; Tom Watson's much the same – 5, 6, 4. It was the Spaniard to play first. His tee shot wasn't what seemed needed. It was well left and in the rough. Seve was disgusted. He was safe enough for a 5 but the Road bunker lay in wait and, if he avoided that, his line to the green was not good. At an angle, this was a narrow target. He'd probably run through and onto the road itself – not a good position to be in.

Well it all came off. Instead of playing for the front of the green and hoping to get down in two from some thirty or forty yards, he went for the heart of the green with a full 6-iron from a rather flying lie. His ball bit and held. He had a certain 4 and minutes later putted up stone dead.

But it wasn't over yet. Immediately behind, Watson hit one of the best tee shots seen all week to the ideal position down the right side, making the Road hole green as easy a target as possible. He paused before leaving the tee, asking if his shot was in bounds. Yes, it was that close, almost in the semi-rough.

Ballesteros saw where Watson's ball had finished. Mentally, he conceded the American a par-4. He would have to birdie the last and that would probably give him the championship by one stroke.

Watson now proceeded to make that result far more likely. From his ideal position, his second shot with a 2-iron was too strong. He hit the green but his ball then careered away, down the bank, across the road and up against the wall, not much more than a foot away.

He had to improvise a shot, going well down the grip and trying to jab his ball towards the pin off the back foot. With so impossibly short a backswing, it ruled out having any feel for the shot.

He managed it well, but not well enough. His ball was on the green but ran well past the flag. His 5 was inevitable and gave Seve a one-stroke lead.

Ahead, the Spaniard drove well and then played a gentle pitch dead on line for the flag which stopped perhaps three yards or so short. There was a pause while Langer, after blowing kisses to the vast crowd, ran his putt in for his first birdie since the 10th, a round of 71 and a total of 278, three strokes better than Jack Nicklaus's score in the last St Andrews Championship in 1978. The German had become a man to reckon with in the major championship. He would be rewarded the following spring at Augusta.

Ballesteros by now knew that a birdie 3 would give him the title, barring a miracle or two. He still had to avoid three-putting, however, for that would have him in a tie with Langer. He mustn't be overbold and miss a short one coming back.

His putt was perfect for pace all the way – but not for line. It always looked as if it was going at the right lip. So it was, but that gentle pace meant that his ball toppled in.

Joy unrestrained. Seve thrust his right arm again and again and yet again skywards, no Anglo-Saxon reserve in the gestures at all, and part of the reason why he is such an exciting player to watch.

But just possibly it wasn't all quite over. Ian Baker-Finch, now struggling to break 80 and feeling almost an intruder in these great events, and Tom Watson had still to finish. Watson did make a show of it. He needed a 2 to tie, and before he played his pitch to the green walked all the way up first. His ball was good for line but over the flag. It was all over, one of the greatest championships of the past several years. As Seve said in his improving English: 'I feel very exciting.' He certainly was.

In that same victory speech he referred to Tom Watson. It had been nice to beat 'in my opinion number one in the world'. Was he being polite or did he actually believe it? I think Seve has thought himself the best player since around 1982, but there is no doubt in my own mind that this championship meant that Seve had won the battle for supremacy.

Results in 1985 confirmed this. Watson won nothing, failed to make the Ryder Cup team and finished well down the US money list in eighteenth place. Some say the defeat at St Andrews has affected his confidence as badly as Tony Jacklin's trauma at Muirfield in 1972. How sweet it would have been to become the only player other than Harry Vardon and Jack Nicklaus to win one of the four major championships six times! He no longer expects to get half a dozen ten-yarders a tournament or sometimes in a single round. In 1985 he was just trying to get it close, and tried three different putters and as many putting strokes in the attempt.

Ballesteros, on the other hand, at times seemed able to win as he pleased, and though many felt that Bernhard Langer just about had the edge on the season's results it was, as the Duke said, 'a damned close-run thing'. There may be a new battle for supremacy between Spain and Germany, but for the moment Langer has much still to do and Seve is the bookies' choice every time he cares to play.

13

The Championship Returns

In Victorian and Edwardian days, there was no doubt at all that British golfers led the world – and by a very long way. At the forefront from the mid 1890s onwards was that great threesome of Vardon, Taylor and Braid. It became almost a freak of nature if another player won a tournament or a championship if these three were in the field.

In the twenty-one years from 1894 to 1914, for instance, only five other players won the Open Championship and one of these, Sandy Herd in 1902, had the advantage of using one of the first wound balls to appear in Britain when the rest of the field were still using gutties. No 'foreigner' was given a second thought, though Arnaud Massy caused some raised eyebrows by winning the championship at Hoylake in 1907 by two strokes from J. H. Taylor.

Although he was the first player from overseas to do so, he was a familiar figure and no one seriously considered the Frenchman the superior of Vardon, Taylor and Braid or, indeed, several other British players. It was just 'his' year, that's all, and afterwards he retreated a rung or two down the ladder. Even so, the French, with Massy himself, Louis Tellier and Jean Gassiat in their ranks, were perhaps the premier golfing nation after the British. No one gave the Americans as much as a second thought. All their best players seemed to be Scottish: emigrants from Carnoustie, Prestwick, Dornoch and St Andrews and the other great centres of the country's golf.

However, there were straws in the wind. Johnny McDermott in 1911 became the first American-born US Open Champion and repeated the feat the following year, still under twenty-one years of age. In 1913, Francis Ouimet, an amateur, only a few months older than McDermott had been creating tremendous excitement by defeating Harry Vardon and Ted Ray in an eighteen-hole play-off for the title. Both these Americans decided to try their hand at the British Championship but caused little stir. McDermott did well to tie for fifth place in 1913, but finished eleven strokes behind the champion, J. H. Taylor. Ouimet was a massive twenty-six strokes behind Harry Vardon the following year. British was obviously still best.

In the American Championship, however, the portents were clear with the American-born Walter Hagen, and the amateurs Jerome Travers and Chick Evans winning in successive years before the First World War called a halt.

When the First World War ended, Vardon, Taylor and Braid were all close on fifty. Their day was over, though Taylor in fact continued to feature for some years. At least two players, George Duncan and Abe Mitchell, were left to carry on the great traditions.

However, the almost total eclipse of British golf was at hand and Walter Hagen and Bobby Jones were soon dominating the championship. In the 1930s there were signs of a revival as Henry Cotton, Alf Perry, Alf Padgham, Reg Whitcombe and Dick Burton became champions – but with very few Americans in the field except for 1937, one of Cotton's years.

After the Second World War, Cotton won again in 1948, as did Irishman Fred Daly in 1947 and the Englishman Max Faulkner in 1951. As before American entries were few until the 1960s, but in the 1950s Bobby Locke of South Africa and Peter Thomson of Australia made the championship almost a Commonwealth affair. Thereafter, the destination of the title varied: Australia,

USA, New Zealand, Argentina and South Africa. After 1951 eighteen years passed before it returned to British hands, those of Tony Jacklin, in 1969. For a brief spell, between 1968 and 1972, Jacklin was át his peak and seemed as good as anyone, but when he faded there was no successor.

The 1985 Ryder Cup emphasized, however, that there are now many good British players: Sam Torrance, Howard Clark, Ken Brown, Paul Way, Nick Faldo, Ian Woosnam and Sandy Lyle. Earlier, Faldo and Lyle had shown it was possible to win tournaments in America while Torrance and Brown had come very close. Howard Clark won the individual title in the 1985 World Cup in California, while British teams also performed very well in the Nissan and Dunhill team competitions at the end of the 1985 season. Pre-eminent was the achievement of Sandy Lyle in becoming the first British player to take the Open Championship since Jacklin sixteen years before. Roger Bannister was the first man to break four minutes for the mile; afterwards, this became an every-day feat. Lyle may not win another championship, but I believe he is the first of a new wave. They will certainly not win every year but Lyle has shown it can be done, like Bannister before him and the first climbers of Everest who have had so many successors.

These are my memories of what happened at Royal St George's during a few days in July 1985.

On the first day there was a medium breeze helping on the early holes. Trevino, full of confidence, went to two under par after three holes and just as quickly lost the two strokes gained on the 4th, a monster par-4 of 470 yards. Peter Jacobsen, however, managed to birdie that hole and got to the turn in 31, four under par and particularly pleased that a little grip change seemed to be doing the trick. He dropped a shot on the 13th, and then came to the tee of the Suez Canal hole, where an out of bounds tight along the right had already given trouble. In a threeball consisting of Howard Clark, Tom Kite and Vicente Fernandez, only Clark had kept his ball in play,

Fair enough. Our club has never invited an American to play in our monthly medal!

Kite sending one out of bounds and taking 7 while Fernandez was in the end pleased to move on with an 8 on his card after hitting two tee shots out.

Jacobsen aimed well away from the out of bounds towards rough along the left. It wasn't the answer because his ball was lost, and he followed with a correction that *was* out of bounds and a third tee shot that took some finding in the rough. His eventual 9 meant four strokes lost to par on one hole. He did wonderfully well to finish with a 71.

The star of the day was Christy O'Connor Junior, who didn't par a hole until the 11th. He began by three-putting the 1st for one-over-par 5, birdied the 2nd and three-putted again at the 3rd. However, there were single putts at the 4th, 5th, 6th, 8th and 9th for an outward nine in 30, and he followed immediately with another birdie – 33 for ten holes with two bogeys on his card. O'Connor was level par for the remaining holes to be in with 64 and leader at the end of the first day by four strokes.

Sandy Lyle, round in 68, had played as well as anyone and felt that his score was just about the worst he could have done with some half a dozen putts missed from six feet or less, including one of not much more than a foot on the 1st hole. Lyle felt very confident with his driving, which had been helped by a club once owned by Irishman Eamonn Darcy, but often contented himself with flicking his tee shots 250 yards or so with his 1-iron. He had some luck as well, chipping in for a birdie on the 13th and holing a very long putt on the 15th to save his par. He finished with a very good 4 at the 18th, one of the most difficult holes on the course with a good drive, a splendid iron shot from a sidehill lie and two putts.

This is how they stood at the end of the day:

O'Connor   64
Lyle, Philip Parkin, Tony Johnstone, Robert Lee
and David Graham   68
David Whelan, Billy McColl, Gordon Brand
Junior, D. A. Weibring and Fuzzy Zoeller   69

I don't think it would be unkind to say that at least

half a dozen of these had no chance of being champion and perhaps only three were men to risk money on – Lyle himself, David Graham and Fuzzy Zoeller. However, you can never tell. Seve Ballesteros arrived from nowhere in the 1976 Championship where he led the field after three rounds. Was it possible that youngsters such as Brand, Lee or Parkin could make a run at the championship? Lyle, however, was probably thinking far more of the pre-championship favourites who were Ballesteros, overwhelmingly, followed by Bernhard Langer and Tom Watson. Ballesteros had done his cause no good at all with an opening 75. Although he won at Royal Lytham in 1979 after a 75 in the third round, this one was compiled in fairly good conditions for scoring. Langer and Watson were closer at hand, but had conceded four strokes to Lyle. Langer was hurt by a 7 on the par-4 15th, when he drove into the face of a bunker and was still five yards from the hole after five shots. Watson began his campaign with a hook from the 1st tee and a thinned third shot through the green. He ended with a 6 on this par-4. Thereafter, he kept to par. Even so, there was talk that his putting was giving him trouble, the feature of his game that has both saved, and made, so many of his scores. Was it ominous that Tom had abandoned his Ping putter and was using a Zebra in public for the first time?

On the second day the weather was bleak: strong winds, rain and waves racing in across Pegwell Bay. It was so unpleasant that twenty-three players scored 80 or worse, but most of the leaders coped well enough with the conditions, the most severe since 1974. For the first time ever Jack Nicklaus failed, his rounds of 77 and 75 causing him to miss qualifying by three strokes. O'Connor began to stumble early on, reached the turn in 40 and had seven bogeys in his first fourteen holes played. As so often, the first-round leader looked on his way out of contention just as quickly as he had arrived. Not so this year, for O'Connor was in very good form. He rallied and finished the day with a 76 and, after a pair of 72s over the last thirty-six holes, was to finish just a couple of strokes behind the champion.

The round of the day came from Bernhard Langer, a 69 played in the worst of the weather when the true par was perhaps 74. He dropped shots on the 16th and 18th only, and was established as the new and firm favourite on 141. Ballesteros was gone, following his 75 with a 74 and making the thirty-six hole cut with nothing to spare. But the Spaniard played some inspirational golf on the third day and a round of 65 or 66 began to look possible until he dropped shots on the closing holes and finished in 70. Lyle's start was disastrous – two shots dropped on the very first hole, where he was plugged in a bunker and took two shots to get out, and then he dropped another at the 3rd. All this was highly uncomfortable with the 470-yard 4th hole, into the wind, just ahead. Lyle got past this in par and then picked up three birdies in the remainder of the outward nine. He was level par for the day and back in business. One over par on the second nine was good scoring, and his 71 left him tied for the lead with Australian David Graham on 139, close behind were:

> Christy O'Connor, D. A. Weibring and Tony Johnstone   140
> Wayne Riley, Emilio Rodriguez, Ian Woosnam, Peter Senior, Robert Lee, Howard Clark and Bernhard Langer   141

On the third day Sandy was out last with David Graham, though they stopped when thunder, lightning and torrential rain caused suspension of play for about an hour. However, all the leaders enjoyed better weather than the early starters. Both Graham and Langer covered the first nine in 33 while Lyle's putting began to look frail. He began to fall behind, with bogeys on the 10th and 11th. In the end, two good shots saved him. The first came at the 17th when he had played three shots to this par-4 and was still not on the green. His ball was on a downslope in the semi-rough and fifteen yards or so from the pin. From here Lyle played a deft little pitch stone dead and got away with a bogey 5 when a 6 was all too likely. Minutes later, he had a putt of some five or six feet to save his par on the last. Few of his keenest supporters expected him to make it but down it went, plumb in the middle. With his 73, he had lost some ground while Langer, improving all the time (72, 69 and 68), was joint leader at the end of the day:

Langer and Graham   209
Lyle, Woosnam, Mark O'Meara and
O'Connor   212
Tom Kite (after a third-round 67) and Peter
Jacobsen   213
Greg Norman and D. A. Weibring   214
Payne Stewart, Mark James, Bob Charles, Anders
Forsbrand, Graham Marsh, Fuzzy Zoeller and
Robert Lee   215

No one was looking much further for a winner than Bernhard Langer, the year's Masters Champion and twice second in the championship, in 1981 and 1984. If he faltered, surely David Graham, the only Australian to win the US Open, and also a former PGA champion, would be the man.

Certainly either of these two, with a three-stroke lead, would need some catching. A low round from someone would be necessary. Lyle himself thought he would only stand a chance with nothing worse than a 68.

There were indeed several rounds under 70, almost entirely from players out of close contention. The Spaniard José Rivero had a 68 and it took him into third place. Another came from the American Payne Stewart, the year's steadiest player in the four major championships. This was a far more significant score. He was home and dry, leader in the clubhouse on 283, when the front runners still had many holes to play. As time went by it began to look as if the twenty-eight-year-old, whose standard dress is plus-twos, argyle stockings and cap, might find himself the winner or in a play-off if the errors out on the course continued.

These began on the 1st hole, a par-4 of 445 yards. Lyle, Graham and Langer each discouraged himself by dropping a shot. Such errors, even if only for a matter of minutes, suddenly made Tom Kite the leader by a clear two strokes. He went to the turn in 32, but then self-destructed on the 10th where his second shot missed the green, his third was struck a little heavily and rolled back into a bunker and his fourth was thinned through the green into rough. Kite did well to get down in two more, but it was a 6 and his chance was gone. In the event he took 40 on the last nine holes. Tom Kite must have been in with a chance of victory in a score of major championships and has not won one. Some *just* win. Kite seems to be one of those who just can't.

Behind the battle was on. Lyle was playing steadily.

After that bogey on the 1st Lyle parred the remainder of the outward nine having picked up a birdie on the 7th, a par-5 easily reachable in two by the whole field on the final day.

Langer, on the other hand, had four 5s in the first six holes, none a par-5, and one came on the 6th, a par-3 of little more than 150 yards. However, he hit back on the 7th hole with an eagle 3 but still took 39 to the turn. It was all drifting away. To give himself a chance, he needed to be under par on the more difficult second nine.

David Graham's bid for the championship was also tentative. He dropped shots on three of the first five holes, but birdied the 7th to be out in 37. A birdie followed on the 10th and it began to look as if, with Langer failing, the Australian might take charge. Despite his errors, he had only momentarily been out of the lead. At the 11th, a par-3, both he and Langer were bunkered from the tee. Langer got down in two; Graham didn't. A couple of holes ahead, Lyle dropped his first shot for a long time.

The Australian still led at one over par from Christy O'Connor at two over. At three over par were Lyle, Stewart (safely in the clubhouse) and Langer. A multiple play-off looked the most likely end to the day – unless one of the players still out on the course made a decisive move.

That move was imminent and it came from Sandy Lyle. At the 14th he drove well left to avoid the fatal out of bounds, but was well down in the rough and could only wedge out short of Suez, the canal that really makes the 14th, only 508 yards, a testing par-5 for even the best players.

Sandy still had nearly 200 yards to go and needed a 2-iron. His shot was good, and came to rest on the right edge of the green but over twelve yards from the flag. Still, he ought to save his par-5. Instead he holed only his second long putt of the week and drew within a stroke of David Graham, level with O'Connor and one better than the leader in the clubhouse, Payne Stewart.

Better was to follow on the 15th, a long par-4 of 467 yards. He needed only a 6-iron for his second shot, got it to about fourteen feet and holed the putt to go one over par and move into the joint lead.

Sandy knew, as that putt fell, he could win – if he parred the last three holes. There were about a thousand yards to go: 165, 425 and 458. At the 16th he was on the green with his tee shot. He left his first putt a nasty four feet short, but managed to get the next one down. At the 17th he drove into light rough and his second was a little short of the green, leaving him a shot up a slope which he sent about four feet past. Again he took up that rather casual stance and knocked it in.

One to go. A par and the championship could be his – but what a beast of a hole. The players reckon it to be one of the most difficult finishing holes on our Open Championship courses. It is, some of them say, 'unfair', declaring that the green was designed to receive a high shot with, at most, a 6-iron. From the back championship tee, however, a long iron to the green is usually needed.

After a big drive into light rough down the right, Lyle needed only a 6-iron. His approach was good, but the green falls away to the left and so did his ball – into a hollow, through the short grass and into a clump of quite thick rough. Just a few inches, but it made the difference between using a putter and a sand iron.

Perhaps that wasn't the club to use. There'd have been less margin for error if he'd played a stiff-wristed push with, say a 9-iron, but at moments of high tension it's not surprising a player uses the club he trusts the most. Lyle attempted to bump his ball into the upslope in front of him and let it run on towards the pin. Perhaps he wasn't positive enough; perhaps grass got between blade and ball. There's no perhaps about the result, however. His ball pitched into the slope, hesitated and then rolled back almost to his feet. Sandy fell to his knees, beating the ground with his club. Maybe he was putting on a show of anguish for the gallery. He knew he could still be in a play-off with Graham or Langer, or both – if he could get down in two more, not so easy with a slope to come up and nine or ten yards to go. He judged his first putt well, finishing about two-and-a-half feet past, then holing out bravely for his 5. Stewart was beaten. What could David Graham and Bernhard Langer do?

At the 15th Graham had dropped a shot, but Langer had come back into the championship with a birdie. Both needed a par finish to tie Sandy Lyle. Both dropped shots on the par-3 16th as Lyle was finishing his round and that was just about that. Both parred the 17th, so each needed to birdie the 18th to tie. The Australian bunkered his second shot and took 5. Langer struck a high cut shot at the flag which finished five yards off the green on the right. He had to hole a chip for a play-off, and did indeed shave the hole before running about five feet past. When he missed the putt, that man long in the clubhouse, Payne Stewart, was outright second. Sandy Lyle was the first British Open Champion since Tony Jacklin in 1969 and assured of his golfing immortality. Perhaps it wasn't a great championship, but what a great result.